Menam

CHAO PHRAYA

River of Life & Legend

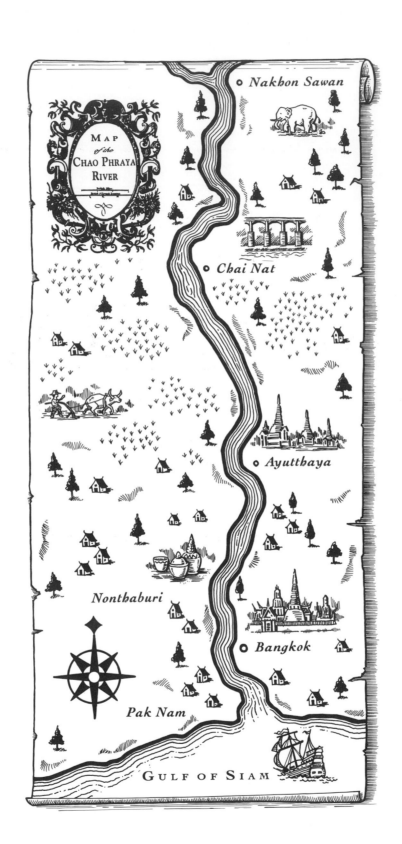

MENAM CHAO PHRAYA

River of Life & Legend

JOCK MONTGOMERY

WILLIAM WARREN

POST BOOKS

co-published by

THE CHAO PHRAYA RIVER CLUB

Acknowledgements

The publisher wishes to thank the following
sponsors for their generous support in helping to produce
this book:

BOONRAWD BREWERY CO. LTD.
CHAO PHYA EXPRESS BOAT CO. LTD.
CITIBANK N.A.
PETROLEUM AUTHORITY OF THAILAND

Thanks also to Vincent Tabuteau of Siam Exclusive Tours
Ltd. for his assistance in this project.

First published by Post Books in 1994 in
conjunction with the Chao Phraya River Club.
Post Books is a division of
The Post Publishing Public Company Limited,
136 Na Ranong Road, Klong Toey,
Bangkok 10110, Thailand.

ISBN: 974-202-022-1

Text © 1994 William Warren
Photographs © 1994 Jock Montgomery

Editor: David Pratt
Designer: Annie Vaillancourt
Map illustrations: Than Theintavat
Additional photos: Photobank, Hataitip Devakul

Printed by: Allied Printers, Bangkok

CONTENTS

$\mathcal{I}$NTRODUCTION

$\mathcal{J}$udged solely by its length, the Chao Phraya River cannot be described as particularly impressive. From its starting point at Nakhon Sawan, at the northern edge of Thailand's Central Plains, it snakes a mere 365 kilometres through a landscape of unremittingly flat farmland before emptying into the sea at Pak Nam. The Ping and the Yom, the two waterways that merge to form the Chao Phraya, are both longer—590 and 555 kilometres respectively—while the mighty Mekong of the north and northeast flows through four countries and covers a total of 4,335 kilometres in its course from the Himalayan mountains to the South China Sea.

But such yardsticks are invariably misleading. Englebert Kaempfer, a German who made a brief visit to the country as a physician on a Dutch ship in 1690, came rather closer to the truth when he noted that "Me Nam, or Meinam in the Siamite Language, signifies Mother of humidities, which name hath been given to this River by reason of the

abundance of its water, which renders the whole Country fruitful."

Menam, which may be rendered more accurately as "mother of waters", is in fact the name given to all rivers of significance in Thailand; but there is no doubt that the Chao Phraya is more deserving of the appellation than any contender. On either side of its relatively short course stretches one of the richest rice-growing regions in the world, a flat, fertile basin protected by rugged mountains or high plateaux on three sides and regularly replenished by layers of silt that are swept down from the highlands. Settlers have been drawn to this tempting abundance since remote prehistoric times; with the emergence of Ayutthaya as the Thai capital in the fourteenth century, it became the stage upon which most of the great events in the national history were enacted, as it continues to be more than 600 years later.

If the writings of early European visitors can be accepted as true, there was some confusion about the course of the Chao Phraya above Ayutthaya. Nicholas Gervaise in *The Natural and Political History of the Kingdom of Siam* (1688) says he was told that "it divides up imperceptibly into a labyrinth of countless branches, in which, if one does not have the secret, one is in danger of getting lost. Indeed, some men who were sent out formerly by order of the king to find the source of the river, which still remains undiscovered, having travelled a long way in their search, were greatly astonished to find themselves back again at almost the same spot as that from which they had started." Gervaise — generally a meticulous observer; he was perhaps the first to point out the general use of the term *menam* for any river — goes on to report: "Some people believe that [it] is a branch of the Indus, others that it springs from the mountains bordering China and Laos. It seems more likely that it comes from a great lake which was discovered some years ago in Laos."

His countryman Simon de la Loubère, who headed a French embassy a few years later, bemoans the fact that the Siamese had no map of their kingdom ("or at least know how to keep it secret", he notes darkly, and perhaps correctly) and also mentions the famous lake. He tends to discount the possibility that it could have existed, however, on the grounds that the river "is so small at its entrance into the Kingdom of Siam [i.e. just above Ayutthaya] that, for about fifty leagues, it carries only little boats capable of holding no more than four or five persons at most".

Kaempfer says that he was told by local people that the Chao Phraya "takes its rise like the Ganges of Bengale in the high mountains of Imaas [i.e. the Himalayas], though it spreads itself into several arms which run through Cambodia, Siam, and Pegu [Burma] into the Sea; and they pretend that these arms are again joined by several smaller branches, not only with each other but also with the Ganges itself". With characteristic precision, Kaempfer notes that he "refuses to stand to the truth of this account; but as for what relates to the description of the River from [Ayutthaya] to the Sea, and the drought I have given of it, this wants no support; forasmuch as I have had sufficient opportunity, and leisure, to observe it myself in sailing up and down".

Modern geographers offer some support for the seemingly fanciful stories Kaempfer was told. According to one theory, cited by Yoshikazu Takaya in a scientific and historical study of the Chao Phraya delta, the Chao Phraya was formerly a river of great length that rose in Tibet and formed a large plain about its lower reaches; it was subsequently "beheaded" by a later river, the Salween, following the principle that when two rivers collide, the younger, more vigorous of the two will capture the upper reach of the older and weaker stream. Evidence for this is provided by the existence of broad gravel beds on river terraces in the far north, forming a perfect link between the two rivers. Takaya states his belief that the old Chao Phraya ceased to exist "several tens of thousands of years ago", but that in palaeolithic times it had been "a major river rising in Tibet and discharging into the Gulf of Siam".

There is also some degree of mystery as to precisely just when and how the river acquired its proper name. In 1850, King Rama IV, the first Thai ruler to become proficient in English, offered the following comment to the *Bangkok Calendar*, a newspaper edited by the American missionary Dr Dan Beach Bradley:

"The word Menam in Siamese is a generic

name for river, and one of the names of the Bangkok river. But as the Siamese call all rivers 'Menam,' and the word is used by them in the same manner as river in English … it is wrong for Americans and some other nations to call the Bangkok river simply 'Menam,' for it has a specific name, same as the Amazon, Ganges, etc. It is the custom of the Siamese to call the stream nearest to them 'Menam,' and add the name of one of the principal towns or villages on its bank to it, as Menam Bangkok, Menam Koung, Menam Tachin, etc. The true name of the Bangkok river is 'Menam Chao Phraya,' but it has become obsolete."

If the name had in fact become obsolete, that rather than the ignorance of foreigners might explain why none of the early writers used it; there remains, however, the question of when it was first bestowed, not to mention of when it may have regained currency.

Whatever its geological origins, the significance of the Chao Phraya in the historical development of central Thailand can scarcely be overestimated. Quite apart from the abundance that it has always provided in the form of fish and nourishment for fields and orchards, it served for centuries as the principal means of communication with the outside world and thus as a means of the trade that made both Ayutthaya and Bangkok such prosperous cities.

Up that busy riverine highway from the gulf to both capitals came a richly varied cast of characters, humble and exalted, aspiring and avaricious, romantic and shrewd. In the early years of Ayutthaya, there were Chinese junks with their teakwood hulls and great bat-like sails, bringing raw silk, quicksilver, iron pans, and fragile blue-and-white porcelain to trade for such valued local products as sappanwood, timber, animal hides, ivory,

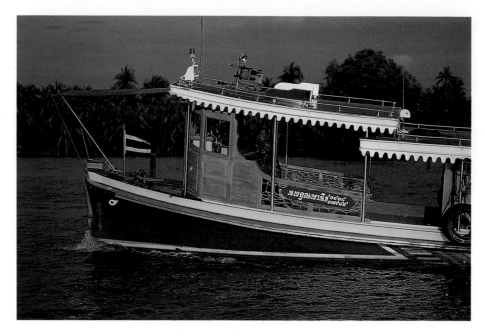

and saltpetre extracted from bat dung (rice did not become a major export until much later). Dependent on winds, they reached the mouth of the Chao Phraya and sailed up with the aid of the southwest monsoon, which blows between May and September, spent the autumn months in the city, and then left with the northeast monsoon. In 1511, one of the junks brought Duarte Fernandez, the first emissary from the scarcely imagined Western world, sent by the Portuguese conquerors of Malacca and graciously received in audience by King Ramathibodi II, to whom Fernandez presented a sword with a golden scabbard, encrusted with diamonds.

Others as well came to the fortified island capital, to partake in its growing prosperity or to bring new ideas to its remarkably tolerant population. They included Japanese fleeing religious persecution in their own country and also seeking their fortune; Persians who settled down and became assimilated; Dutch and English, both official traders and interlopers of dubious repute. Off an English ship in 1675 stepped a brash young adventurer of

THIS PAGE: A typical wooden river tug, used to tow barge trains.
FACING PAGE: A tug sets up a towline for two laden barges while a fisherman goes about his business beside a raft of water hyacinth.
FOLLOWING PAGES: Children seize the pleasures of life on the river; a panoramic view from Wat Arun in Bangkok.

Greek origins named Constantine Phaulkon, who was to enjoy a brief but legendary career as the Thai king's favourite; aboard the *Oiseau* and the *Oriflamme* came envoys and soldiers from the Sun King of France, Louis XIV, among them a witty former transvestite who had assumed the sober robes of a Jesuit priest but whose taste for the exotic remained as keen as ever.

A similarly diverse group crossed the shallow bar at the river's mouth and made the shorter voyage to Bangkok during the nineteenth century: Jean-Baptiste, later Bishop, Pallegoix, a Roman Catholic priest who was to befriend and influence a king; the American missionary Dr Dan Bradley, who would introduce modern medicine and the printing press to the country where he spent most of his life in a largely vain effort to propagate Christianity; Sir John Bowring, the British diplomat who succeeded in negotiating a historic treaty where several of his less tactful countrymen had signally failed; a rather mysterious young woman named Anna Leonowens, with a secret past and a future even her romantic nature could never have imagined; a Polish sailor who later emerged as the writer Joseph Conrad; and countless others, less well known, who also recorded their emotions as they followed the river on its way to what Conrad later called "the Oriental capital which had yet suffered no white conqueror"

All these visitors are part of the Chao Phraya story, part of the tangible sense of romance that still clings to its banks like the mist that swirls over the water in the early morning; and so is the river's equally captivating contemporary life, some of it aggressively modern but much of it timeless—a reflection, indeed, of the kingdom through which it winds its leisurely course, gathering lore and legends all the way.

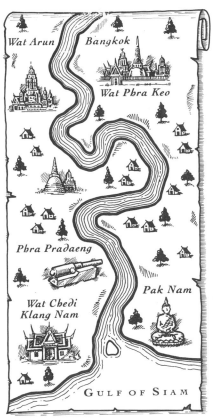

Wat Arun
Bangkok
Wat Phra Keo
Phra Pradaeng
Wat Chedi Klang Nam
Pak Nam
GULF OF SIAM

$\mathcal{P}$ak $\mathcal{N}$am to $\mathcal{B}$angkok

PREVIOUS PAGES: *Fish caught in the Gulf of Thailand being unloaded at a wholesale market on the river.*
FACING PAGE: *Mid-nineteenth century view of Pak Nam at the mouth of the Chao Phraya.*

"Vexations! At daybreak we were under weigh. The pilots thought we should get safely over the bar; but, there being only thirteen feet, we made slow progress through the hard sand, and at last stuck; moved on again—stuck anew; again a little progress; but the turn of the tide made the vessel unmanageable, and we finally found ourselves on the inner side of the bar, but fast in mud and sand. However, the ship has made herself a bed, and does not roll."

Thus Sir John Bowring, Governor of Hong Kong and Minister Plenipotentiary to China, also accredited to the courts of Japan, Siam, Vietnam, and Korea, recorded in his personal journal on 2 April 1855. He was on his way to Bangkok to conduct what proved historic trade negotiations with King Rama IV, and like many travellers before and after him he had almost been defeated by the shallow sandbar at the mouth of the Chao Phraya River.

The river is very wide at this point—one can scarcely see from one muddy bank to the other—and a stream of silt-filled water stains the Gulf of Thailand outward for several kilometres. The silt, especially at the end of the rainy season, brings fertility to the vast Central Plains, one of the greatest rice-growing regions on earth and the location of three Thai capitals. It also accumulates at the river mouth at the rate of some five metres a year, so that Bangkok was once much closer to the sea than it is now; three centuries ago, according to a French source, tides were felt as far up as Ayutthaya and even at Lop Buri on a tributary.

The bar blocking easy access to the Chao Phraya was regarded as a hazardous nuisance by travellers like Bowring. The Marquis de Beauvoir, who arrived aboard a crowded Thai steamer from Singapore in 1867, had an even more alarming experience in the same place. "At low tide," he wrote, "it is only covered with three feet of water. This ridge of sand and mud is completely hidden by a bamboo stockade, like a straight line of fortification, to which are fastened the enormous nets used by Siamese fishermen. We steered through a channel about fifty yards wide, left like a door of entrance to the besieging waves. But it seemed that the aquatic sport has been very great, and some thousands of prisoners were trying to get through the straits we had crossed. Suddenly the engine stopped, without any previous orders. Great confusion on board; terror and anxious inquiries from the three hundred natives. 'Had we touched some rock, and were we about to sink?' Nothing of the sort; it was a whole shoal of fish that were gradually being sucked up by the water into the boiler, and who stuck like living glue in all the pipes and valves.

They were mostly sardines, bold little fish! As you may imagine, we were obliged to sound, and clear the works, before we set the engine going again."

Bishop Jean-Baptiste Pallegoix observed that only the most experienced pilots were able to steer safely across the bar, and a guidebook written in 1904 calls it "a great hindrance to navigation and commerce", as it undoubtedly was in those days of increasingly large ships. Even the relatively small *Oiseau*, bearing the first French embassy to Ayutthaya in 1685, was forced to remain outside, while its passengers were transferred to royal barges sent down from the capital. (Bowring's party was received in the same manner, though in both cases the reason

may have been mainly ceremonial and a desire to impress the distinguished guests.)

On the other hand, the natural barrier was not one that early Thai rulers were eager to remove. Pak Nam, literally "river-mouth", served as gateway to the world, the place where nearly all foreign visitors caught their first glimpse of the Thai heartland on the voyage to both Ayutthaya and Bangkok; at the same time, it was also a potentially vulnerable point, through which other strangers might arrive on missions less desirable to the Thais than trade and diplomacy. As early as 1690, Englebert Kaempfer, heading for Ayutthaya aboard a ship belonging to the Dutch East India Company, saw "some batteries planted with cannons on both sides of the river, which were raised in the late French troubles"—a reference to problems that had arisen two years before as a consequence of the visit by the *Oiseau*.

This danger was particularly felt during the nineteenth century when Thai leaders noted that the British invasion of neighbouring Burma had been carried out largely through its river systems. To the bar were added a variety of more serious man-made fortifications at or near the town of Pak Nam, ranging from conventional forts to a massive metal chain that extended across the Chao Phraya and that one source claims was obtained by ordering every blacksmith in Bangkok to contribute a certain number of links. Perhaps more practical was the use of palmyra trunks driven into the mud to form a crescent, with sufficient room for only two or three ships to pass within range of a gun battery.

Not all visitors were impressed by these precautions. John Gillies, who saw them in 1825, felt that "so flimsy are these airy buildings that they will not long stand the shock of their own guns, much less that of an enemy's". Even after the Pak Nam forts were considerably improved, and others were added further upstream at Pak Lat (now known as Phra Pradaeng), they did not prove to be of much use on the one occasion when they were really tested.

The incident occurred in 1893 during another quarrel between Thailand and France, this time over Laos, when the French demanded permission to send gunboats up the Chao Phraya to Bangkok to reinforce their demands. When this was denied the boats came anyway, silenced the Pak Nam guns in a brief engagement, and dropped anchor near the French embassy in the capital, within ominously close range of the Grand Palace.

The Thais submitted gracefully, despite their resentment; the foreign minister, Prince Devawongse, even made a trip to the waterfront to congratulate the French commander on his bravery in breaching the riverine defences.

PREVIOUS PAGES:
Fishing boats on their way down the river to the gulf, and fishermen bringing in a day's catch.

FACING PAGE: *Fish and dried squid, two popular items of the Thai diet.*

RIGHT: *A fisherman mending his nets.*

The Bang Phli Festival

LEFT: *A parade of boats, part of the Bang Phli Festival in Samut Prakan Province; the Luang Pho Toh Buddha image, almost covered with offerings of lotus blossoms; and spectators at the festival.*
FOLLOWING PAGES: *Boat races at Bang Phli; a boxing match over water; and a steersman on one of the racing boats.*

One of the most colourful annual water festivals is held at the village of Bang Phli on Klong Samrong in Samut Prakan Province. Like the Wat Chedi Klang Nam fair, it takes place in late October, when the rivers and canals are at their highest, and involves both local Thais and descendants of the Mon settlers of Phra Pradaeng.

The focus of the festival is a revered Buddha image known as Luang Pho Toh, enshrined at Wat Bang Phli Yai Nai. Legend claims that it was one of three golden images thrown into the Chao Phraya by residents of Ayutthaya when the old capital fell to the Burmese in 1767. The images floated in the river for many years before two of them were discovered by villagers in Chachoengsao Province and placed in temples there and in Samut Songkhram; the third and largest was rescued later and taken to Bang Phli.

During the festival the image is placed in a boat and carried along the canal at the head of a gala procession, steadily acquiring an ever-growing mass of lotus blossoms thrown by people along the route as offerings.

In addition to its solemn religious aspect, the celebration also offers ample opportunities for Thai-style *sanuk*, or fun. There are the exhilarating boat races that accompany almost every water-oriented festival, as well as boxing matches fought on poles suspended over the canal, folk theatre performances, and a competition to select the most beautifully decorated boat in the procession.

LEFT: *One of the guns that once defended Pak Nam from invasion up the river.*

PAK NAM is today officially known as Samut Prakan, and while one of the old guns can still be seen on the left bank, the modern town on the right would be unrecognisable to any of the old visitors with its extensive customs house, its multistoreyed harbour control headquarters, its clock towers, and its fleet of fishing boats plying the broad expanse of choppy water. Near shore the noise of traffic can be clearly heard, sometimes accompanied by amplified music. Above a fringe of palm trees in the distance rise the landmarks of the Ancient City, a huge outdoor museum with replicas of historical Thai monuments, and nearby is the Crocodile Farm, a popular tourist attraction.

A very different scene greeted John Crawfurd, sent by the governor-general of British India to lead a trade mission to Thailand in 1822. Crawfurd's reception at Pak Nam was far less warm than he had expected, which perhaps accounts in part for his description of the town as a "long, straggling, and poor place" and his unfavour-able comparison of the governor's residence with the cottage of an English peasant. Anna Leonowens found the customs house to be nothing more than "an open sala, or shed, where interpreters, inspectors, and tidewaiters [pilots] lounge away the day on cool mats, chewing areca, betel, and tobacco, and extorting money, goods, or provisions from the unhappy proprietors of native trading craft, large or small".

Others, too, had a less than happy first impression. The American missionary Dr Dan Bradley, arriving thirteen years later and forced to remain outside the bar for eight days due to tides, wrote that his heart sank when he saw "the degradation of the inhabitants of Pak Nam and their despicable filth. ... We could not but wonder how long we should be permitted by God to live in such a pagan land as this."

Nor was Bradley much taken with the governor, who received him lying on a sofa clad in a loincloth, with one leg over the back and the other

RIGHT: *Statue of King Chulalongkorn in the Royal Thai Navy fort at Pak Nam.*

stretched out. "Among the many questions the Governor propounded," the virtuous missionary recalled, "was whether we had brought along any spirits, saying he wanted a little for the purpose of compounding some medicine. … He suffered from a constitutional stomach ache, effectually to cure which he begged very hard for two bottles of English brandy, offering to give us a small detachment of chickens and ducks in return. We were informed by Brother Johnson [a fellow missionary] he had learned to love the taste of brandy from Europeans and Chinese coming into port, and that the spirit question he put to us was the one always uppermost when he greeted foreigners."

It is only fair to note here that Bradley's disillusionment with Thailand was short-lived. Though he failed signally in his efforts at Christian conversion, he went on to spend the rest of his life in Bangkok, where he became an influential friend of King Rama IV, introduced modern medicine, and established the first printing press.

Still a prominent sight across from the town, however, is the graceful spire of Wat Chedi Klang Nam, "temple of the stupa in the middle of the river", rising some thirty metres high from a cluster of trees on the west bank. Construction was started in 1822 by order of King Rama II, to let sailors know that they were entering a Buddhist country, and completed under King Rama III in 1828. Once, as the name suggests, it was indeed on a small island some distance from the shore; alluvial deposits, however, have largely filled in the space between, so that today the site is part of the mainland at low tide.

Whatever their misgivings about Pak Nam, almost every nineteenth-century visitor who left an account seems to have been charmed by this first glimpse of the exotic culture they had come so far to see. "The bar passed," wrote Carl Bock, "we came

to a small island in the river, upon which is built a Wat, or temple, … whose gilt spires, … towering far above the tree-tops, shone resplendent in the evening sun. I felt that I was at last in the land of Temples and Elephants, the land where sober truth and strange fiction are so curiously interwoven that it is often difficult to distinguish the one from the other."

Even the apprehensive Anna Leonowens, on her way to educate some of the royal children of King Rama IV (and eventually to fame, a century later, as the heroine of *The King and I)* was dazzled by what she deemed to be "perhaps the most unique and graceful object of architecture in Siam, shining like a jewel on the broad bosom of the river, a temple all of purest white, its lofty spire, fantastic and gilded, flashing back the glory of the sun, and duplicated in shifting, quivering shadows in the limpid waters below".

The English Governess

Of all the Westerners who sailed up the Chao Phraya, undoubtedly the best known to the world at large was a 31-year-old (not 28 as she claimed) Englishwoman named Anna Leonowens, who with her small son Louis crossed the bar at Pak Nam aboard a small Thai steamer late in the afternoon of 15 March 1862.

She had been engaged to teach English to some of the wives and children of King Mongkut (Rama IV) and she remained in the kingdom for five years, leaving on the same steamer that had brought her in July of 1867. "All our European friends accompanied us to the Gulf of Siam," she wrote in the first of the two memoirs she later published, "where we parted, with much regret on my side. ..."

The fact that only her "European friends" apparently saw her off is instructive. It is doubtful that the king much regretted her departure (in a letter that same year written to the Siamese vice-consul in Singapore he complains of her audacity and tendency to meddle in his affairs), nor, probably, were her students greatly upset. In fact, Anna was not all that popular during her Bangkok stay except in American missionary circles and, in the words of Alexander Griswold, "a cool assessment reveals that she did not loom very large in the life of King Mongkut or his children".

This is not, of course, the impression given in her memoirs, or in the best-selling *Anna and the King of Siam,* adapted from them by Margaret Landon in 1943. Most of all, it is not the one carried away by the countless thousands who

delighted in *The King and I* on stage and screen. The Anna that emerges in these, especially the last, is a plucky young gentlewoman of noble Welsh birth, still mourning the loss of her husband, a British officer, and determined to bring good to a country languishing in the darkness of pagan belief and polygamy.

The truth of her background, not revealed until the 1970s by a biographer of her son Louis, was somewhat different. Anna, he discovered, was born not of distinguished parents but to a lowly English soldier in India and a mother who was probably Eurasian. The dashing young soldier she claimed to have married was, in fact, a clerk named Thomas Leon Owens who ended his life in 1859 as a hotel operator in Penang.

Even before she arrived at Pak Nam, Anna was busily reinventing herself—probably not the first or the last to do so in these exotic surroundings. Her performance may not have been as flawless as Deborah Kerr's in *The King and I,* which could explain her rejection by the old British colony in Bangkok. The American Protestant missionaries, though, took her at her word; and, no doubt gratefully, she adopted the prejudices that coloured their views of Thailand and royal polygamy.

One other aspect of Anna's secret life is equally intriguing. Erasing her past meant a clean break with her sister Eliza in India. Thus Anna may never have known that Eliza's daughter also married a Eurasian and that the youngest child of the union ultimately became the actor Boris Karloff, the monster of Frankenstein fame.

Anna Leonowens, whose memoirs inspired The King and I.

RIGHT: *Wat Chedi Klang Nam, scene of a popular annual festival.*
FOLLOWING PAGES: *Villagers draping the stupa with a sacred cloth, a highlight of the Wat Chedi Klang Nam Festival.*

Characteristically, she tempered her admiration with a less charitable comment on the land where she would spend five years: "A charming spot, yet not one to be contemplated with unalloyed pleasure; for here also are the wretched people, who pass up and down in boats, averting their eyes, pressing their hard, labour-grimed hands against their sweating foreheads, and lowly louting in blind awe to these whited bricks."

The modern river traveller might dispute Anna's architectural assessment of Wat Chedi Klang Nam—as he certainly would her view of the "wretched people"—but there is no denying the beauty of its site or the elegance of its central spire, which is now ungilded. Once a year, usually in late October or early November depending on the lunar phase, the temple is the scene of a festival during which a large cloth is ritually wrapped around the stupa by neighbouring people and colourful boat races are staged in the Chao Phraya and some nearby canals.

A somewhat cynical guidebook written in 1904 by one J. Antonio asserts that the fair is "really in the nature of a kind of harvest thanksgiving because at this season, the upcountry rains being practically over, the rice and other crops show the promise of coming out well, whilst the waters, coming downriver, irrigate the low-lying alluvial plain on which Bangkok stands. Hence all cull out a holiday, the maidens don their brightest robes and costliest jewels whilst the youths paddle about in long snake-like craft and the vendors of sweet-meats, cakes, and the like enjoy a highly profitable time of it. It is possible, however, that were the upcountry crops to show no prospects of good whatever, the festivities would be held all the same for the Siamese is not ultra particular about such matters and enjoys life whenever he can."

AFTER PAK NAM, the Chao Phraya leads to Bangkok in a series of great swooping curves, at times almost doubling back on itself and increasing the distance between the two considerably. Early Ayutthayan kings had seen this winding course as strategically useful, delaying approach while defences could be raised should an enemy attack by that route. Later, however, as trade increased, the time lost became more of an annoyance and in 1722 a canal about one kilometre long was dug by 10,000 conscripted labourers to eliminate a particularly large loop near the present-day town of Phra Pradaeng. The canal reduced the journey by seventeen kilometres but had the unfortunate side-effect of allowing salt water to go up the river as far as Bangkok in the dry season. Still later, after the establishment of Bangkok, Thailand's first railway was built to Pak Nam in 1893, making it possible for visitors to reach the capital in an hour or so after being ferried ashore from their ships.

Phra Pradaeng, the next important town, stands on the west bank of the Chao Phraya. It was known to early travellers as Pak Lat. In late Ayutthayan times a Dutch trading post called Fort

Amsterdam was located just below this point. When Kaempfer arrived there in 1690 on one of the few European ships that were allowed in the kingdom after the French had been expelled two years earlier, he was well received by a man whom he describes as "the Governor of that place, one Core, a Swede by birth".

The fort itself, according to Kaempfer, was "built according to the fashion of the country on piles of bamboo. Stores of deer and buffalo skins were kept in lofts, but the red wood [sappanwood] for dying … lies in an open place till ships come to take it in, which happens every year, and the greater part of it is carried to Japan. … This wood rubbed with some lime and water yields the finest violet colour one could wish to see. This mixture is said to cure some eruptions on the skin."

Despite his civility, the slightly mysterious Core—how did a Swede come to be manager of a Dutch trading post in remote Siam?—was grieving over the loss of a tame jungle cat, "which he found

PREVIOUS PAGES: *An ice factory on the river; and a barge being unloaded at one of the many waterside warehouses.*

ABOVE: *An early nineteenth century view of Phra Pradaeng, then known as Pak Lat.*

LEFT: *A view of the mid-river fort and temple commented on by almost every visitor to early Bangkok.*

FACING PAGE: *Locks leading to a short-cut canal near Phra Pradaeng.*

FOLLOWING PAGES: *A boatman on the river.*

again … but in the belly of a snake he had killed, and which, as he complained, had robbed him before of many of his hens, having always been lurking in corners, under the houses".

The fort eventually fell into ruins and crumbled into the river where, hidden at high tide, it still presented a danger to navigators at the time of Crawfurd's 1822 visit; the Marquis of Beauvoir saw it, too, and referred to it contemptuously as the "Dutch Folly". Today it seems to have vanished completely, though no doubt some of its bricks still lie deep in the mud along the bank.

Pak Lat was established early in the Bangkok period, principally as a second line of defence in case of attack from the sea. Its proper name at the time, bestowed by the king, was Muang Khuan Khan, though most foreigners continued to call it Pak Lat, just as they called the capital Bangkok even after it acquired a much grander title. The original settlers were some of the Mon families who had fled Burma in the 1770s and had been given permission to live at Pathum Thani, further upriver. According to Dynastic Chronicles, the first group moved by royal order to Pak Lat consisted of 300 adult men between twenty and thirty years of age and their families; the city pillar was installed on 2 June 1815, and later that same year more Mon refugees entered the country and were assigned to the new town.

Bishop Jean-Baptiste Pallegoix, who visited it in the 1830s, says the people of Pak Lat earned a living by supplying Bangkok with rice, vegetables, and charcoal made from the mangrove trees that grew plentifully along the river-bank. Shortly afterward, F.A. Neale found it "very prettily situated. Close to the water's edge are neatly built cottages of the artificers and others employed in the construction of canoes, and at the time of our visit there was a state canoe being constructed for His Majesty, of a length not less than from seventy to eighty feet. … The little homes in the central part of the town were principally occupied by husbandmen and farmers. Each house was detached, and had a garden containing trees yielding the most luscious fruits in the East, and many rare and beautiful flowers."

The settlement was also heavily fortified against potential invaders. Sir John Bowring and his party, having been transferred to a squadron of splendidly carved royal barges for their approach to the capital, were shown "enormous and formidable chains and wood-work which had been made to protect the river, and which at one time, we were informed, might be used to stop our progress: but, instead of an impediment, we found a major-general, wearing gold and silver flowers on the side of his round cap, he being clad in a jacket of purple silk with gold ornaments, and telling us he spoke Portuguese, and was descended from Portuguese ancestry, but he had never left Siam".

No such figure is likely to be encountered in modern Phra Pradaeng, a bustling community that stretches along the west bank, its economy boosted by workers from factories located a few kilometres upstream and at first glance suggesting little of its past. Closer inspection, however, reveals the square Mon facial characteristics of many of the people, a bungalow-style district office festooned with Victorian fretwork, and a castellated little fort, complete with guns, that has been turned into a pleasant riverside park. Phra Pradaeng is particularly lively at Songkran, the Thai New Year celebration in April, when crowds come from Bangkok and even further to watch lavish boat processions, release fish to make merit, and join in free-for-all water throwing.

Songkran Festival

One of the most exuberant festivals of the Thai year is Songkran, which celebrates the traditional new year over two or three days in mid-April. Like many others, this is a blend of solemn ritual and *sanuk,* or fun, and involves the use of water at several stages during the course of its observance.

Houses are thoroughly cleaned on the morning of the first day, and younger members of the family pour lustral water over the hands of elders as a sign of respect. Other activities take place outside the home, particularly in and around Buddhist temples. To make merit, people build small stupas of sand, called *chedi-sai,* in the monastery compound and release fish in nearby rivers and canals. The principal Buddha image is ritually sprinkled with water, either inside the temple or, in large cities, as it is carried through the streets as the centrepiece of a splendid procession accompanied by elaborate floats.

Once the ceremonies are over, Songkran assumes a boisterous, carnival-like atmosphere as young and old take to the streets and happily throw water on one another in the belief that a thorough soaking will bring a bountiful supply of rain to farmlands in coming months; some simplify the process by going to the nearest river for an all-out splashing to ensure maximum results. Since the event falls at the height of the hot season, the impromptu bath comes as a welcome relief as well as one of the ultimate expressions of uninhibited *sanuk.*

While Songkran celebrations take place throughout the country, some have become especially noted for their high spirits, among them the one staged by the Mon people of Phra Pradaeng on the lower Chao Phraya. This takes place several days later than the Bangkok Songkran and attracts large numbers of visitors who arrive by road and boat to enjoy its varied and festive activities.

FACING PAGE:
Songkran traditions.
Making sand stupas in
a temple courtyard
during the Songkran
Festival; paying respect
to a Buddha image;
releasing fish to acquire
merit; pouring lustral
water to show respect to
elders.

RIGHT: *Annointing a*
Buddha image as part of
the Songkran Festival
at Phra Pradaeng; and
presenting offerings to
monks, another impor-
tant Songkran activity.

FOLLOWING PAGES:
Water throwing, a
popular part of the
traditional Thai
New Year celebrations.

ABOVE: *A woman and child enjoying the cool river breezes.*

RIGHT: *Fishermen on the river against a background of nipa palms, still widely used as a roofing material.*

FOLLOWING PAGES: *A man cleaning one of the ubiquitous river barges.*

ABOVE Phra Pradaeng, it is difficult to reconcile old accounts with the scenery along the Chao Phraya today. There are, it is true, still long stretches of nipa palms growing out of the water—they provided most of the thatching for Thai houses in the past—fleeting glimpses of bird life in occasional clumps of trees, and the soaring, multi-tiered roofs of Buddhist temples. More prominent, however, are the busy factories of one of Thailand's first modern industrial complexes, from which goods can be loaded directly on to ships for export and among the employees of which, perhaps, are descendants of those Phra Pradaeng artificers whom Neale encountered; plastic bags, chunks of styrofoam, and other disposable aspects of contemporary life litter the river surface; and one never has the sense of isolation and unspoilt nature that so impressed visitors from the Ayutthaya period through much of the nineteenth century.

It is strange, therefore, to read the observations of the Jesuit priest Nicholas Gervaise, made in 1688: "The water of the river is extremely clear, light, and excellent to drink; during the rains it becomes somewhat muddy and then it quite often causes dysentery, unless care is taken to guard against this by allowing the water to stand in great jars made especially for the purpose, in which it loses this bad quality."

To Bowring, nearly two centuries later, the river was "beautiful, crowded with the richest vegetation to the water's edge. Now and then a bamboo hut is seen amidst the foliage, whose variations of bright and beautiful green no art could copy. Fruits and flowers hang by the thousand on the branches. We observed that even the wild animals were scarcely scared by our approach. Fishes glided over the mudbanks, and birds either sat looking at us as we passed, or winged their way around and above us. The almost naked people sat and looked at us as we glided by; and their habitations were generally marked out by a small creek, with a rude boat and one or more pariah dogs."

Animal life seems to have been plentiful, not all of it harmless. "In the less frequented parts of the river," Gervaise wrote, "one often encounters enormous crocodiles, which are hostile to humans and fish alike. As the Siamese cannot refrain without great discomfort from frequent bathing, scarcely a year passes in which some unfortunate is not devoured by these monsters." Kaempfer also complained of being unable to take very long walks near Fort Amsterdam, since the woods were "infested with Tygers and other voracious beasts", although this was more likely due to scare stories passed on by the grieving Core than to reality.

Less intimidating to Kaempfer were the "incredible number of monkeys of a blackish colour, some of which are of a very large size, and some less of the common sort, and a grey colour, which walk about tame, and as it were for pleasure sake along the shore, or climb the trees. ... The she ones hold their young so fast on their breasts that they would not let go, even when they were shot down."

Fish were equally abundant. The most common, according to Gervais, was "18 inches long and 10 or 12 inches wide and it has a rather flat and almost square head. There are two kinds, one ash-grey in colour and the other, which is better, black. To preserve it, it is dried in the sun and, because it is highly valued in neighbouring countries, the Siamese do a great trade in it. The Dutch are most partial to it and acquire it from Batavia; they eat it instead of Mayence ham. The fish in the river are not at all similar to ours, but those who, like myself, have eaten them cannot deny that they have a much better taste."

The Invisible Scourge

The deadliest of all invaders arrived at the mouth of the Chao Phraya unseen, crossing the natural barrier without difficulty. Cholera came from India and first struck Thailand in the far south at Nakhon Si Thammarat. It reached Pak Nam, probably aboard a ship, in 1819; dozens of people died, causing others to flee to Bangkok and elsewhere and thus contributing to the rapid spread of the disease.

It returned the next year as well, with even more terrifying results. The people of Bangkok viewed it as some supernatural curse, as suggested by the Royal Almanac: "On the 7th month, the waxing moon, a little past 9 o'clock in the evening, a shining light was seen in the north-west and multitudes of people purged, vomited, and died." According to Dr Malcolm Smith, "so many were dead that the temples could not dispose of them fast enough. Like logs of timber, so the record runs, the corpses lay stacked in the grounds, and many more were left to float about in the river and canals. It was a visitation that the people had never known before. They fled in panic from the city; the monks deserted the monasteries; the whole machinery of government came to a standstill."

Some association of the pestilence with water was recognised, and the royal court had special water brought from Phetchaburi, eighty kilometres away, where it was collected from a clear stream and sent by boat to the palace. For the general public, however, the Chao Phraya was the capital's only water supply; and cholera continued to be an annual scourge from April to July, when the river was lowest. It varied in severity; one of the worst years was 1849, when between 15,000 and 20,000 died in a single month and at Wat Saket, where the poor could be cremated at government expense, bodies had to be left exposed to pariah dogs and vultures; but each season took its grim toll.

"The European treatment with astringents, opium, and alcohol was not much better than that used by us in the Middle Ages," wrote Dr Smith. "It was no more successful than the treatment given by native doctors whom we despised. ... In those days death claimed its victims swiftly; one evening you sat with your friend, and the next evening you went to his funeral. In the heat of the tropics, the dead do not keep nicely."

Control finally came with construction of the Bangkok Waterworks in 1914 when, at least for the majority, the Chao Phraya ceased to serve as a source of drinking water.

LOWER LEFT: *The grave of a Danish sailor who succumbed to cholera in Bangkok early this century.*

ABOVE: *Unloading tapioca at a godown, a familiar sight on the lower Chao Phraya. Tapioca is now one of Thailand's leading exports.*

a minute. Every flash somewhat resembled a flash of lightning, except that the light was spangled with innumerable bright spots, from which the light emanated. At length, one part of the chain lost its time, and then another part, until they had broken into some three or four companies harmonising in their own groups but not as a whole band."

Neale, too, was enchanted when his boat became entangled with foliage on the bank and, pulling away, dislodged "myriads of glittering fireflies that ever and anon sparkled forth ... throwing upon the water and all around one bright transcendent glow of radiant light".

For some unknown reason, fireflies are seldom seen on the Chao Phraya today and never in the dazzling quantity described by Dr Bradley and others. One older Thai resident of Bangkok, who remembers seeing them in his youth, thinks they were attracted to a particular kind of shrub that once grew along the river profusely but that has been killed off by increasing salinity of the water; in support, he claims to have planted some surviving specimens of the shrub in his garden and to have been rewarded with at least a modest display.

Still all too plentiful, however, is another nocturnal insect that attracted attention. "As the banks of this great river are densely populated and permanently covered with some of the most beautiful greenery in the world," wrote Gervaise, "it would be a very great pleasure to sail on it, if one were not tormented from sunset to sunrise by a small army of mosquitoes, which follow one everywhere. These creatures prefer to attach themselves to Europeans than to natives, because their blood is better and their flesh more delicate. ... The only way of protecting oneself against them is by making a smoke screen or by hiding one's whole body under a muslin net."

Neale records being awoken at night by a loud throbbing beat he thought came from native drums, despite no sign of habitation. "This noise arose, as I afterward learned, from a species of fish that followed in the wake of the vessel, and which ... are termed by the Siamese the Drum Fish. I saw some specimens of them afterwards in Bangkok: they are very ugly, with a species of bladder under the throat (from which the curious sound is emitted), and wholly unfit for food."

One of the most memorable of the sights on the lower Chao Phraya, mentioned by many travellers, was the spectacle of what Dr Bradley called "the far-famed fireflies of the Menam" when night fell. "They were playing on the trees that lined the banks of the river," he wrote. "There was an unbroken chain of them for some ten rods, all flashing their phosphorescence in concert about sixty times

Bangkok

Bangkok

BANGKOK

"There it was, spread largely on both banks, the Oriental capital which had yet suffered no white conqueror; an expanse of brown houses of bamboo, of mats, of leaves, of a vegetable-matter style of architecture, sprung out of the brown soil on the banks of the muddy river. It was amazing to think that in those miles of human habitations there was not probably half a dozen pounds of nails.

"Some of those houses of sticks and grass, like the nests of an aquatic race, clung to the shores, others seemed to grow out of the water; others again floated in long anchored rows in the very middle of the stream. Here and there in the distance, above the crowded mob of low, brown roof ridges, towered great piles of masonry, king's palace, temples, gorgeous and dilapidated, crumbling under the vertical sunlight, tremendous, overpowering, almost palpable, which seemed to enter one's breast with the breath of one's nostrils and soak into one's limbs through every pore of the skin."

The author was an obscure, thirty-year-old Polish seaman named Teodor Konrad Korzeniowski, who when he gave up the sea for literature became Joseph Conrad—a change that not only simplified things for countless future students but also for Bangkok's Oriental Hotel, which named a suite in its author's wing after him.

At the time of Conrad's visit, in 1888, the "Oriental capital which had yet suffered no white conqueror" had served as the seat of government for barely more than a hundred years. It had been known, however, for much longer than that as one of the major stops on the busy river route to Ayutthaya.

The name derives from *bang*, meaning village, and *kok*, a species of wild plum (*Spondias pinnata*), which apparently grew in some quantity at the site. A settlement so called was known to the early Portuguese, who made their first official contact with Ayutthaya in 1511 and a few years later signed a Treaty of Friendship and Commerce. The main course of the Chao Phraya at the time was the large loop which is today formed by the Bangkok Yai and Bangkok Noi canals. At the beginning of his reign in 1534, to provide a short-cut for the increasing number of ships coming to the capital, King Phrajai ordered a canal dug to join the ends of

PREVIOUS PAGES: *Bangkok riverscape.* **THESE PAGES:** *River scenes in Bangkok a century ago.*

the loop, a distance of about three kilometres; within a few years, water flowing through the new channel had so widened it that it became the main stream, the section now overlooked by the Grand Palace.

King Mahachakpat (1549-1569) raised the status of the village to that of a town and, at the same time, changed its name to Thon Buri. The new name won little acceptance from European visitors, who continued to call it Bangkok; eventually, Thon Buri came to mean only the settlement on the west bank.

According to European missionaries in the seventeenth century, Bangkok was actually a collection of villages, noted for their plantations of tall areca-nut palms; the main one, with the governor's house, was on the west bank of King Phrajai's now broad canal, across from today's palace. The site was undeniably strategic "the only place that could offer some resistance to enemy attack", according to Nicholas Gervaise—and later in the same century two forts were built there, one on the west bank at the mouth of Klong Bangkok Yai and the other slightly downstream on the east bank.

The Chevalier de Chaumont and his aide the Abbé de Choisy, leading the historic embassy sent by King Louis XIV, spent an evening at Bangkok in October 1685. They were proceeding by stages up the Chao Phraya to Ayutthaya in a fleet of barges sent by King Narai, stopping each night at a guest house especially built for them.

"Half a league from Bangkok," wrote Choisy in his journal (throughout which, incidentally, the name is spelt Bangko), "two important mandarins, one of whom is Portuguese, came to receive the Ambassador, with many barges, so that the procession gets bigger every day, and will do so until reaching the city of Siam [i.e., Ayutthaya]. The Portuguese has come to take command of the troops in Bangkok, and will be above the Governor. At

Bangkok there are two forts on either side of the river. … As soon as we appeared, an English vessel, anchored there, greeted the Ambassador with a seventeen gun salute. The two forts saluted too, one with thirty cannons and the other twenty."

When the party left the next morning, "the two forts saluted us with all their guns firing. We noticed that in front of all the villages along the river

BELOW: *View of the ever-changing modern Thai capital.*
FACING PAGE: *New building rising on the river, a characteristic sight in Bangkok today.*

bamboo walls covered with greenery had been built, an honour reserved for the King alone. We were to find the same thing right up to the city of Siam. All the houses for the Ambassador were painted red, another particular mark of honour. Both banks of the river are edged with betel-nut palms and coconut trees, which are green and laden with fruit, monkeys, and birds. Some birds are all blue, others all red, still others entirely yellow. The prettiest are the egrets, which are completely snow-white and have on their heads a true aigrette spray. There are many animals in this land, because people dare not kill them in case they kill their father; metempsychosis is an article of faith among the Siamese."

Three years later, following an upheaval that will be examined more fully in the section on Ayutthaya, French troops made a last stand at Bangkok in the fort on the east bank. Thai forces occupied the west bank fort and harassed the enemy with artillery fire and flaming arrows aimed at the thatch-roofed buildings in the camp. When one of the junior French officers attempted to get down-river in a small boat to summon aid from ships waiting in the gulf, he was surrounded by Thai craft; allowing them to come near, he then detonated an explosion that killed himself, his crew, and many of the attacking Thais.

A truce was eventually reached whereby the French were allowed to leave; Kaempfer in 1689 found their fort "quite demolished", but noted that apart from this "the banks above Bangkok are pretty well inhabited, and stocked with houses and villages".

PREVIOUS PAGES: *A* hang yao, *or long-tail boat, commonly seen along the river; smaller boats, useful for navigating the shallower canals.*

LEFT: *Boatmen taking a rest during a quiet time on the river.*
FACING PAGE: *Repairing the propeller of a long-tail boat; a* hang yao *making waves, and noise as well.*

Chao Phraya river express

The story of the ferry boats on the Chao Phraya begins, rather improbably, with an aristocratic beauty from northern Thailand and extends over three generations of female ownership.

Khunying Boonpan arrived in Bangkok toward the end of the nineteenth century as an attendant of Chao Dararasmi, a Chiang Mai Princess who became a consort of King Chulalongkorn. In time, she married and left the Inner Palace, settling in a house on the Chao Phraya with her husband and six children. It was there, in the 1920s, that she decided to buy a few simple rowing boats and start a cross-river ferry service to earn a little extra money.

Khunying Boonpan's youngest daughter, Khunying

Supatra Singholaka, later took over the business and introduced the first motor boats. Then and for the next forty years the Supatra Company operated only ferries between Thon Buri and Bangkok; in 1971, it acquired the government-operated service up and down the river, now known as the Chao Phya Express Boat Company, stopping at piers built and maintained by the company on both banks.

Today the company is headed by one of Khunying Supatra's daughters, Supapan Pichaironarongsongkram, and still thrives with a fleet of twenty-eight boats that operate during daylight hours between the Krung Thep Bridge and Pak Kret. A popular day-long cruise up-river to Bang Pa-in Summer Palace is offered every Sunday.

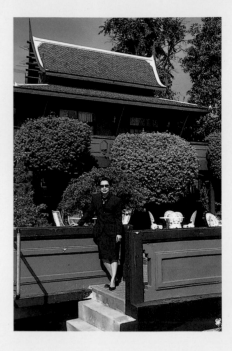

ABOVE: *Khun Supapan Pichaironarongsongkram, present manager of the Chao Phya Express Boat Company, at the house where her mother lived on the river.*
LEFT: *Prasert Thongkham, who has spent most of his life operating a cross-river ferry.*
FACING PAGE: *Express and cross-river ferry boats, filled with rush-hour passengers.*

BANGKOK re-entered Thai history in a significant way following the fall of Ayutthaya to the Burmese in 1767. Amidst the confusion of defeat, in which the old capital was almost totally destroyed, a former governor of Tak Province emerged as a charismatic military leader. Within less than a year he had expelled most of the remaining Burmese and established his headquarters at Thon Buri; shortly afterward, having subdued rival Thai leaders elsewhere in the country, he became King Taksin.

Much of King Taksin's rule was spent consolidating his power and adding to his territory. There was little time to transform Thon Buri into anything resembling the splendours of the former capital; apart from a number of Buddhist temples—some of which, like Wat Arun, dated from the Ayutthaya period—almost the only reminder of its brief glory are a few ruins that were part of the royal palace, now in the compound of the Royal Thai Navy at the entrance to Klong Bangkok Yai, where the French fort was also situated.

FACING PAGE: King Taksin's palace, now in the grounds of the Royal Thai Navy.
BELOW: One of Bangkok's old forts, now restored, at the mouth of Klong Bangkok Yai.
FOLLOWING PAGES: Wat Phra Keo, the Temple of the Emerald Buddha, at night with the triple-spired Grand Palace beyond; and various scenes within the temple compound.

King Taksin, whose behaviour had become increasingly eccentric, was succeeded by one of his commanders, Chao Phraya Chakri, in 1782. The new ruler, generally referred to as King Rama I, decided to move the capital across the river to Bangkok, partly because the site was thought to be less vulnerable to a Burmese attack from the west—the eastern flank was guarded by a low-lying swamp known as the Sea of Mud, now a fashionable residential area—and partly out of a determination to recreate, as closely as possible, the lost Ayutthaya.

A canal, the present Klong Lord, had already been dug by King Taksin on the east bank at a point where the river curved sharply, creating an artificial island which was further fortified with a wall. Since he deemed the area too small for his planned capital, King Rama I had the wall demolished and a new canal, 7.2 kilometres long and 20 metres wide, dug to the east by a labour force conscripted from Cambodia and Laos; a strong new wall extended along the inner side, 3.6 metres high and dotted with sixteen gates and sixteen forts.

The riverside site selected by the king for his palace was occupied by a prosperous Chinese trading community; this was removed about three kilometres south, outside the city walls but still on the river, and became the nucleus of today's Chinatown.

Work on the palace took three years, with the king himself living on the site in a simple wooden house to supervise the small army of labourers and artisans. Of this endeavour, Prince Chula Chakrabongse has written: "The labour used for the building scheme was conscript or corvee, but it is unlikely that they suffered great hardship. They were fed at the royal expense by a communal kitchen, and some might have had better and more food than at home. If there was much hardship,

some of the stories would have survived. But even if we grant that forced labour, with threats of punishment, was employed for building the new capital, the architects, craftsmen, and skilled artisans, who embellished these buildings, could not be coerced by fear into producing such beautiful works of art. Judging by what we can still see today, even if a lot of it has been restored, these men must have been profoundly inspired and stirred by love for Rama I himself as much as for the glory of Thai culture, to have accomplished so much of it in the space of three years."

The palace compound, originally covering an area of 21 hectares—another 3.5 hectares were added to the south by King Rama II in 1809—faced north, with the Chao Phraya on the left. It was divided into various parts, just as the palace in Ayutthaya had been. The outer area contained the civil and military headquarters, along with the royal guards; in the central portion were the king's living quarters and the audience halls where he received visitors and presided over royal ceremonies; and connected to the rear of these was a well-guarded area where the female members of the royal family lived with their numerous attendants. In another part of the compound was the royal chapel, formally known as Wat Phra Sriratana Sasadaram but more usually called Wat Phra Keo, the Temple of the Emerald Buddha. The high surrounding walls had seventeen gates, the principal one being Pratu Wiset Chaisi, "The Gate of Glorious Victory", in the centre of the north wall.

Celebrations to mark official completion of the palace in 1785 lasted three days, during which pavilions serving free food were set up in the area and monks chanted prayers from the heart-shaped battlements on the city walls. The revered Emerald Buddha—a jadeite image of northern Thai origin, which Rama I had brought back from Laos—ceremonially crossed the Chao Phraya from its temporary home at Wat Arun and was installed in Wat Phra Keo, amid a profusion of rich offerings and glittering architecture that symbolised the young Chakri dynasty's cultural vitality.

Just outside the palace walls, Rama I installed the Lak Muang, or city pillar, which is to be found in every provincial capital and generally marks the exact geographical centre. Derived from Brahmin custom, this is believed to enshrine the city's guardian spirit and has ever since been an important place for worship by the people of Bangkok.

As a final act, the king bestowed an impressive new title on his capital, one so filled with honorifics that it qualifies as the longest city name in the world. Thais simply call it Krung Thep, which can be roughly translated as "city of divinities or angels", while foreigners (and most foreign map makers) have continued to use the old name.

Rattanakosin Island, as it is called, formed the heart of early Bangkok, the source of all spiritual and temporal power, with the Chao Phraya as its vital artery. Along the river came food and other supplies from nearby provinces; trading ships came as well, together with many new inhabitants, particularly Chinese, full of energy and ambition. Like Ayutthaya, the city was planned principally in terms of water transport; and to this end new canals were built to facilitate communication. At least one served another purpose as well; when he ordered construc-tion of Klong Mahanak, which extended eastward in a straight line near the present Golden Mount, Rama I specifically noted that it was intended as "a place where the people of the capital city could go boating, singing, and reciting poems during the high-water season, just like the custom observed in the former capital of Ayutthaya".

Looking back in old age on all the changes that had taken place since his arrival, Dr Dan Bradley recalled that in the early nineteenth century, "there was not one square-rigged vessel belonging either to the Siamese or the Chinese. The native commerce of the Kingdom of Siam was carried on entirely by means of junks of Chinese fashion, of all sizes of tonnage from five-hundred down to fifty tons. The largest junks plied between Bangkok, Singapore, and Batavia; while the smaller traded to the ports belonging to Siam along the eastern and western coasts of the Gulf. Junks in the China trade would then as now make but one voyage in a year, taking advantage of the favouring southwest monsoon in June to sail from Bangkok and of the northeast monsoon to return the latter part of January or the first part of February. From February to June there were annually from 60 to 80 of these monsters of the deep moored in the river, forming two lines, all heading down stream, always ready as to position to start on another voyage.

"These two lines of junks were practically a great bazaar for a period of two months or more from the time of their arrival. … The goods they brought from China were chiefly teas, silks, crepes, cotton fabrics, paper, crockery, Chinese cutlery, Chinese trunks, betel boxes, Japan woodware, mirrors, and a thousand smaller objects of Chinese manufacture. The junks from Batavia and Singapore brought cotton goods, flannel and other woollen fabrics, glassware, and European cutlery."

PREVIOUS PAGES: *Guards arriving at the Grand Palace landing for a royal ceremony; and the Grand Palace enclosure, as seen from the Chao Phraya.*

FACING PAGE: *Late nineteenth-century views of shipping on the river, then the heart of Bangkok.*

Klong life

FACING PAGE: *Scenes along the canals of Thon Buri. An orchid nursery; unloading sand dredged from the river; canal-side transport; preparing offerings at a Chinese shrine.*

RIGHT: *An artist at work in a waterside house.*

Old houses along the river

FACING PAGE:
An old, garden-fronted royal residence; the French Embassy with its own landing stage; a

former Chinese residence on the Thon Buri bank, now a boy's school; and the cream-coloured face of the old Bank of

Thailand building, formerly a royal residence designed by a German architect.

ABOVE:
Wat Ratchathiwas, where King Rama IV served as a monk.

MISSIONARIES formed a prominent part of the nineteenth-century Bangkok scene. The tolerant Thais, secure in their blend of Buddhist, Brahmin, and animistic beliefs, had never placed any serious obstacle in the way of proselytising on behalf of other faiths; and many Roman Catholics had come to Ayutthaya for that purpose. They were not very successful — the Thais were amazed by the infighting between different groups — and caused active offence by their efforts to convert King Narai, but except for one brief period they were allowed to practise freely.

The Catholics were also the first in Bangkok and built a number of churches along the Chao Phraya that can still be seen rearing Gothic spires amid the modern skyscrapers. Among the most influential was the learned Bishop Jean-Baptiste Pallegoix, who resided for a time at the Church of the Immaculate Conception near the present Krung Thon Bridge. The future King Mongkut was then a monk at nearby Wat Samorai (now Wat Ratchathiwas) and the two became friends, exchanging language lessons and discussing theology as they strolled in the evening beside the river.

The first Protestant missionaries, an Englishman and a German, arrived in 1828 and were the ones with whom the Portuguese consul sat under the tamarind tree in his riverside garden. Others soon followed, including the remarkable Dr Bradley, who stepped ashore in July of 1835 after a lengthy voyage from Boston and six months in Singapore waiting for a ship that would take him on the final lap of his journey.

Initial impressions were not encouraging: "When I rose on the first morning in Bangkok and took a glance of things around me, I could scarcely resist the sense of foreboding that assailed me. Oh how different, I thought, was the natural scenery here from what it was in Singapore. How gloomy the dwellings of the missionaries here when compared with the charming house we had occupied on that attractive island. …

"There was no prospect that seemed even the least cheering but the river, and that was so shut out from our view that we could see only a very little without walking out on an uninviting footpath to it. There was not even the slightest hill to be seen in any direction. … There were some trees about the place, where thousands of crows came to roost at night. The kakawa kakawa jargon they made in jabbering together in the early evening and morning was such that I had never dreamed of. This noise alone I could have borne without the thought of a murmur, but when united with an incessant jumbling of crickets, toads, and frogs, the barking and howling of dogs, and the snarling of cats, I confess that my missionary home seemed, for a little time, too horrible to endure."

But Bradley was by nature an optimist, and he quickly overcame his despair and began the work that would bring him lasting renown in his adopted homeland. During his first year he treated more than 3,500 patients in his dispensary and performed Thailand's first surgical operations; he later introduced vaccination against smallpox as well as modern obstetric methods. As one of his biographers has noted, "Fame did not come to Bradley in the privacy of sterilised operating rooms under ideal conditions; it came on a simple table in the middle of his office. Privacy was an unknown luxury, for his operations, watched by multitudes of onlookers, served as Bangkok's version of a Hollywood extravaganza." In 1844, he started the *Bangkok Recorder*, Thailand's first newspaper, and in 1858 began publishing an almanac, the *Bangkok Calendar*, to which his friend King Mongkut contributed

FACING PAGE: *First Presbyterian Church, founded in 1860 but rebuilt in 1910, the oldest Protestant church in Bangkok.*

FOLLOWING PAGES: *An area filled with nipa palms, recently reserved as a "green belt" for Bangkok; a midstream tune-up for Madonna Turbo.*

occasional entries. (Another influential friend was Chao Phraya Sri Suriyawong, who became regent when the young Prince Chulalongkorn succeeded to the throne in 1868.)

He also got a more suitable house, near the entrance to Klong Bangkok Yai in the old Portuguese settlement. It was a two-storey bungalow with verandas on all sides and louvred shutters, a style that was becoming common among foreign residents along the river. He was particularly proud of his doors and windows, which he called "a great improvement on all their predecessors, being many and large, with posts plumb, and not leaning together or within after the then universal custom of Siam." Bradley died in 1873, his wife twenty years later; their daughter Irene continued to live in the house until her own death in 1941, after which the property reverted to the Thai government and is now part of the navy compound.

While King Mongkut sometimes quarrelled with the American missionaries, especially on the subject of royal polygamy, he was generally on good terms with most of them and even asked three of their wives to teach English to ladies of the Inner Palace. Among the teachers was Mrs Stephen Mattoon, who left a record of the experience:

"At the river-house [near the palace] we were met by an elderly servant, who received our basket of books and whatever we had to carry, and led us through the windings of the way to our appointed place of teaching. … Here were assembled the king's young wives and princesses of the blood. Curiosity and a desire to please the king brought them together, and lessons in English were made the order of the hour. As was expected these royal ladies dropped away from the English class, and ere long none were left excepting a few young wives who were ambitious to please His Majesty

and to be able to converse with him in English. As the ladies left the class, they wished us to visit them in their homes; which we did, taking with us our Christian books in Siamese, which some of them were fond of reading."

It was the Christian books, and the insistence of the missionary ladies on using them, that eventually led King Mongkut to terminate the classes and, several years later, ask his consul in Singapore to find another teacher. When one was suggested and accepted, he wrote her a formal invitation which, despite the quaint language, leaves no doubt regarding what the king considered to be her duties in the palace.

LEFT: *Divers bringing up bags from the river mud.*
FACING PAGE: *Workers sifting finds in a colander as another diver surfaces.*

"MADAM: We are in good pleasure, and satisfaction in heart, that you are in willingness to undertake the education of our beloved royal children. And we hope that in doing your education on us and on our children (whom English call inhabitants of benighted land) you will do your best endeavour for knowledge of English language, science, and literature, and not for conversion to Christianity; as the followers of Buddha are mostly aware of the powerfulness of truth and virtue, as well as the followers of Christ, and are desirous to have facility of English language and literature, more than new religions.

"We beg to invite you to our royal palace to do your best endeavour upon us and our children. We shall expect to see you here on return of Siamese steamer *Chao Phraya.*"

The teacher, of course, was Anna Leonowens, and her "best endeavour" would be the subject of much future controversy and bitterness; for a fuller discussion of her background see the panel in the first chapter of this book. As she came up the river in 1862, she later wrote: "The sun was already sinking in the west, when we caught sight of a tall roof of familiar European fashion; and presently a lowly white chapel with green windows, freshly painted, peeped out beside two pleasant dwellings. Chapel and homes belonged to the American Presbyterian Mission. A forest of graceful boughs filled the background; the last faint rays of the departing sun fell on the Mission pathway, and the gentle swaying of the tall trees over the chapel imparted a promise of safety and peace, as the glamour of the approaching night and the gloom and mystery of the pagan land into which we were penetrating filled me with an indefinable dread."

Anna never quite lost that unnecessary sense of dread, nor her flair for making the mundane melodramatic, and both pervade her unreliable memoirs that later became the even more unreliable *The King and I.* She was befriended by the American missionaries, however, and Bradley liked her—she offered to testify on his behalf when the French consul sued the *Bangkok Recorder* for libel—though, as he wrote, "I could have wished that she had appeared more frequently at church on Sunday." After her departure she wrote him from Staten Island, New York, asking about the new king, Chulalongkorn, who had been one of her students; the letter closed with the words, "Bangkok is the most hideous word I have ever written or uttered."

Vendors on water

PREVIOUS PAGES: *A worker stands on logs brought to sawmills in the city, with the Rama IX Bridge beyond; and riverside workers buy their lunch from a passing vendor boat.*
THESE PAGES: *Vendor boats on the Chao Phraya, offering goods that include coffee, fresh pineapples, noodles, and betel nut.*

LEFT: *Tapioca moving from a barge to a godown.*
FACING PAGE: *A barge labourer.*
FOLLOWING PAGES: *Workers unloading lumber from barges.*

FEW OTHER foreign visitors of the time shared Anna's sentiments. For most, arrival in the distant Thai capital was coloured by a sense of high romance, a sentiment that is reflected in one of Joseph Conrad's early autobiographical short stories entitled "Youth". The hero, told that his ship is to carry a load of coal from England to Siam, exclaims: "Bangkok! I thrilled. I had been six years at sea, but had only seen Melbourne and Sydney, very good places, charming places in their way — but Bangkok!"

It was the riverine aspect of the city that made the greatest impression. In the 1840s, some ninety per cent of the population lived in what Neale described as "a long double, and in some parts treble, row of neatly and tastefully painted wooden cabins, floating on thick bamboo rafts",

FACING PAGE: *A popular restaurant on the river; passengers disembarking from a cross-river ferry.*
THIS PAGE: *The Chao Phraya by night in central Bangkok.*

while most of the rest lived in structures on stilts along the river and canals. Each floating house was typically three bays deep, the front facing the river and equipped with removable panels; a waterside veranda served as a bathing area in the morning and evening and a shop during the day; while the middle bay was for sleeping and the one near land for cooking.

The houses were fastened by chains to huge poles driven into the river bed and could thus be easily moved when desired. Sometimes the shift was inadvertent, as on one occasion when a passing ship came too close:

"The tide was running down rapidly and so soon as the brig disentangled herself, away went these houses at a steamer's pace, admidst the vociferous hooting and shoutings of their tenants; and

before many minutes had elapsed they had disappeared around a corner of the river, and were stranded on the opposite shore; but they sustained no great injury, for, with the simple difference that their dislodgement was involuntary, this was after all nothing but the method adopted by the natives themselves when desirous of changing the position of their shops. If the air of the 'Fleet Street' of Siam does not agree with Mrs Y and her children, or they wish to obtain a more aristocratic footing by being domiciled higher up and nearer to the King's palace, then all they have to do is to wait till the tide serves, and loosening from their moorings, float gently up towards the spot they wish to occupy."

Also memorable were the incredible royal barges that appeared on the river from time to time, bearing the king to ceremonies at important temples. "They are some of them one hundred and twenty feet long," wrote Bowring, "scooped out of the trunk of a single tree. The prow, rising high aloft, represents the head of a serpent, a dragon, a fish, a deity, a monster, or any fantastic object. The poop, which is also elevated high above the water, is like the tail of a bird or fish, but generally ends in wavy points." The earliest of these fantastic craft dated from the reign of Rama I and represented another of his efforts to evoke the grandeur of Ayutthaya, where such processions had also been among the features that dazzled Western visitors.

The more permanent sights along the riverbanks were equally exotic. "Hundreds of pagodas rear their gilded spires to the sky," wrote the Marquis de Beauvoir, "their innumerable domes inlaid with porcelains and glittering crystals, and the embrasures polished and carved in open work. The horizon was bounded to left and right by sparkling roofs, raised some six or seven stories, enormous steeples of stone work, whose brilliant coating

dazzled the eyes, and bold spires from 150 to 200 feet in height, indicating the palace of the king, which reflected all the rays of the sun like a gigantic prism. The first general view of the Oriental Venice surpassed all we could have hoped for in our travellers' dreams. We longed to get into gondolas and

FACING PAGE:
An independent speedboat
ferrying passengers.

ABOVE: *A cruise boat*
heads for the Memorial
Bridge, the first to span
the Chao Phraya.

Bangkok

Bangkok.
Siam

E. Hildebrandt

go through the lively canals which are the streets of this floating town, and where the bustle, animation, and noise bewildered us."

Water was such a part of daily life that Sir John Bowring thought "the existence of the people of Bangkok may be called amphibious. The children pass much of their time in the water, paddling and diving and swimming, as if it were their native element. Boats often run against one another, and those within them are submerged in the water; but it seldom happens that any life is lost, or mischief done to the persons whose boats are run down. I have again and again seen boats bottom upward, whose owners have floated them to the shore, or otherwise repaired the damage done as speedily as possible. The constant occurrence of petty disasters seems to reconcile everybody to their consequences."

Resident foreigners, on the other hand, were not always so sanguine about the Chao Phraya. The swift tides could be dangerous to a less skilled

FACING PAGE: A view of old Bangkok with Wat Arun in the distance.
BELOW: Early twentieth century postcard showing the royal barges.

Royal State Barge, Siam.

swimmer, or to a drunken sailor who happened to fall from his ship, and the Protestant cemetery on the river-bank has numerous gravestones that attest to the fact. Dr Bradley recorded one near-tragedy when Brother Johnson, a fellow missionary, was saved by his hat:

"Against the advice of many people he decided, one evening, to try his hand at paddling his boat about the river. This is something that no person should attempt if he cannot swim, because if an accident occurs none will come to your rescue. Mr Johnson ignored the warnings and set out in his boat half an hour before dusk. Just as he had got about three hundred yards from shore, his boat jolted up against the cable of a ship, and in an instant was overturned.

"Johnson, who could no more swim than a stone could, had instinct enough to cling to the canoe, and it and the luckless man floated down with the tide. In vain did he shout for aid, and each time he opened his mouth gallons of water rushed down his throat; and so he came to the wise decision to hold his peace and trust to Providence.

"By a most fortunate circumstance Mr Hunter happened to be coming in the opposite direction in a larger canoe. … It was now almost perfectly dark, and Hunter would have passed on without paying the slightest attention to so common a sight as a capsized canoe except that his sight was attracted to something of monstrous dimensions floating behind the boat. He immediately recognised it as the large blue felt hat that Johnson, in common with all the missionaries, wore for protection against the sun. Immediately backing his canoe, Hunter picked up the luckless victim more dead than alive, and conveyed him to his house where, under my attention, he was very soon put to rights again."

LEFT: *The Reclining Buddha at Wat Po, Bangkok's largest temple.*

FACING PAGE: *Monks studying in one of Wat Po's many courtyards; gold and black lacquer decoration on a door at Wat Po.*

BANGKOK would continue to be centred on the Chao Phraya for the better part of the next century, but already developments were taking place on land. A Treaty of Amity and Commerce signed between Siam and the United States in 1833 had brought hope but little in the way of any real trade to the kingdom; when Sir John Bowring arrived in 1855, he noted (obviously ignoring the Chinese) that "all that remained to represent foreign trade was one English (half-caste) merchant, one Armenian, and a few Anglo-Indians from Bombay and Surat".

This changed dramatically as a result of the treaty concluded between Bowring and King Mongkut. It quickly led to agreements with other Western countries, and two years later 200 foreign ships called at Bangkok. Rice became a major export for the first time, mainly to British India, along with other commodities like teak and sugarcane. Embassies and trading companies followed, and soon the city had a sizeable population of Europeans, most of whom lived and worked on or near the river.

They were not as enchanted by water travel as some of the romantic visitors and even petitioned King Mongkut on the subject. According to Prince Chula Chakrabongse in his historical account of the Chakri Dynasty, "Western people had been accustomed for their health to take the air of an evening riding in horse-drawn carriages, and owing to the lack of suitable roads in Bangkok, they were suffering bad health and illnesses. The king said he was grateful for their complaints, and added that he felt ashamed of the dirt and filth of the narrow lanes of Bangkok, and he began a road and bridge building programme."

Charoen Krung, or New Road as it was known to foreigners, is usually described as the first

LEFT: *King Rama IV, better known to Thais as King Mongkut, who set his country on the path to modernisation.*

proper Bangkok street but actually it was preceded by what is now called Rama IV Road. In 1856, Western merchants proposed that a trading community be established some distance from the city near the present-day Phra Khanong with a canal leading to the site. Klong Hua Lampong was accordingly dug and the soil excavated piled up along its north bank to make a road; the merchants then refused to move, on the grounds that it would be too far from Bangkok. In 1861, New Road was built, using earth from a canal dug to link Bang Rak and Hua Lampong canals.

Among the foreign traders attracted to Bangkok was a young Danish sailor named H.N. Andersen, who came first at the age of 23 in 1872 and a few years later for a much longer stay. He was placed in command of a royal Thai sailing vessel, the *Thoon Kramom*, carrying trade goods from Bangkok

From a Proclamation by King Rama IV
on water pollution in Bangkok

RIGHT: *Dead fish and other debris in the Chao Phraya.*
BELOW: *Workers collecting litter from the river.*
FOLLOWING PAGES: *River pollution today, arising from a variety of sources.*

By Royal Command, Reverberating like the Roar of a Lion, Be it declared to all servants of the Crown of higher and lower rank and to all the people of the Realm as follows:

Whereas it has been brought to the attention of His Majesty that ... the inhabitants of the City Divine are great polluters of water, for it is said that the Divine City dwellers do dishonour to their own City by throwing carcasses of dead animals into the rivers and canals where they float up and down in great abomination, and having thus contaminated the water, the City dwellers themselves do make an inelegant habit of constantly using the same water for purposes of drinking and ablution;

Wherefore, His Majesty is graciously pleased to advise that under no circumstances whatsoever should any person allow himself to throw a dead dog, a dead cat, or the carcass of any other species of animal into any river or canal, whether big or small. ... By the exercise of a little thought-

fulness it should not be too difficult to perceive that other people using the water along the waterway do object to such exhibition. Were provincial priests from the Lao country and other northern districts or other country gentry to pay a visit to the Divine City and find the said objectionable custom still in practice, they would undoubtedly carry away the impression that conditions inside the City are not as healthy as outside it, the water supply in the City being so unclean as to breed in the dwellers thereof a number of unhappy ailments. The same or similar impressions would be given to Englishmen, Chinese, and all foreign Orientals who come to do business in the Divine City. ...

From now on should any person disregard His Majesty's gracious advice and still allow himself to practise the said inelegant habit as heretofore, he shall, after due testimony being given against him by his neighbours, be conducted in ignominy around the City by the *Nai Amphoe* as a sorry object of warning to others against committing such an inhuman and irresponsible act of water pollution. ...

Given on Wednesday, the 12th of the Waxing Moon of the Second Month in the Year of the Great Snake, being the eighth year in the Decade by the Stars.

Bangkok

to Singapore and Bombay; in 1883, Andersen loaded the holds of the ship with teak—then a somewhat unusual commodity—and took the *Thoon Kramom* all the way to Europe, returning with a cargo of coal. This innovative and immensely profitable venture marked the start of Andersen's career and eventually led to the founding of the worldwide East Asiatic Company.

Andersen also made another notable contribution to the Chao Phraya scene. A small hotel called the Oriental, catering to seamen, had stood on the river-bank as early as 1865; this was destroyed by fire and another, somewhat larger, establishment was built on the site, conveniently near the French consulate and accessible to New Road. Under the management of two Danes, it became well known and by 1878 was advertising "family accommodations, American bar, billiard saloon, baths, boats for hire, and appropriate rooms for private parties". The hotel also witnessed more than a few brawls, for visiting sailors tended to be a rough lot, and even resident foreigners often scandalised the missionary community with their behaviour. "Delirium tremens seems to have rivalled smallpox as the most common disease among Westerners," Dr Bradley observed sadly.

The Oriental entered a new era when it was acquired in 1884 by Andersen, whose offices were located nearby. Deciding that Bangkok was ready for a really luxurious hotel, he tore the old buildings down, filled in the swampy land, and developed an avenue lined with attractive villas leading to New Road. An Italian firm of architects—one of two then operating in the city—was hired to design the new Oriental, which opened in May of 1887 with "forty commodious and well furnished bedrooms", a French chef lured away from the consulate, and a barman named Spider who knew exactly what everyone drank.

The ultimate seal of social approval was bestowed on the Oriental in December, 1890, when King Chulalongkorn (Rama V) came down the river for a private tour of its amenities, after which he visited the nearby Customs House to inspect plans for new wharves and warehouses.

KING CHULALONGKORN, the first Thai ruler to travel abroad, was determined to modernise his kingdom and thereby reduce the danger of colonisation by Western powers who were then taking over most of Southeast Asia. The inadequacies of the Chao Phraya defence arrangements were brought home painfully in 1893 when the French breached Pak Nam's defences and forced his government to cede territory in Laos and Cambodia; but there were other ways to show the world that Siam was not to be regarded as backward and in need of European supervision.

One, perhaps, was the R.M.S. *Maha Chakri*, the 2,500-ton vessel he had built in England. "She was a most unusual ship," wrote Dr Malcolm Smith, "a combination of private yacht with cushioned lounges, velvet couches and innumerable bedrooms, and an up-to-date vessel of war with steel decks, a ram, two fighting masts, and an armament of quick-firing guns. Its designer, though aware that he was building it for a polygamous monarch, could have had no idea of the numbers that were going to be packed into it; nor could he have done any better had he known. It was constructed to hold at most 150 people, including the crew; into it were crowded, when the Court went off on a trip, some 400 or 500. They filled the cabins, they filled the gangways and passages, and when there was no more room for them below, they camped out on deck. The spectacle of the royal yacht as she steamed down the river and across the bar, packed to her limit, was more like an English pleasure steamer on one of her daily trips, than royalty on tour."

King Chulalongkorn was also the first to envision Bangkok as a city in the European tradition, with tree-lined boulevards, parks, and proper bridges over its many canals. To further this dream he embarked on an ambitious expansion programme in the Dusit area, some distance from the river, where he built a new palace and throne hall, both in Western style, and laid out a system of spacious avenues to accommodate the traffic of the future.

The traffic eventually materialised, as any modern visitor can attest, but not during the king's reign and not for a considerable time afterward. When Somerset Maugham arrived in 1923—one of the few, incidentally, not to enter the city by river but instead overland through northern Burma and then by train—he saw the Dusit avenues and found them "handsome, spacious, and stately" but felt that they lacked reality: "There is something stagy about them, so that you feel they are more apt for court pageants than for the use of every day. No one walks in them. They seem to await ceremonies and processions. They are like the deserted avenues in the park of a fallen monarch."

The real life of Bangkok, as he discovered (after a near-fatal bout of malaria in the Oriental Hotel), was still along the Chao Phraya and its adjacent canals:

BELOW: *Bells at Wat Rakhang Kositharam, a temple dating from the Ayutthaya period.*
FACING PAGE: *Library at Wat Rakhang Kositharam, the residence of King Rama I before he became ruler, and recently restored by the Association of Siamese Architects.*

WHAT REMAINS of this city so many found entrancing? To the present-day visitor trapped in one of its endemic traffic jams, engulfed by fumes and noise, the answer might seem self-evident: scarcely anything. Perseverance, however, brings rewards. The visitor in search of the other Bangkok must leave the streets that have replaced most of the old canals, make his way to the Chao Phraya, and there board one of the many boats still readily available at almost any public landing.

At first glance, while movement is undeniably swifter, the river, too, appears to have changed drastically. Instead of rice silos and bungalows, condominiums and hotels seem to tower everywhere, even on the once bucolic Thon Buri side, in a mixture of architectural styles that can only be described as eclectic. Where not a single bridge spanned the Chao Phraya at the time of Maugham's stay—the first opened in 1932, as part of Bangkok's 150th anniversary celebration—there are now eight within the city area, all crowded with vehicles. Except for the temples, almost everything looks new or at least recent: certainly not devoid of life, for the river continues to be busy, but deficient in history, in the romance of nostalgia.

It requires time, a sharp eye, a stop now and then, a certain effort of the imagination; but the Chao Phraya's legendary past is still there and gradually reveals itself to the traveller by water.

Start, for instance, near the Krung Thep Bridge. There on the west bank, between the Royal Garden Riverside Hotel and the three tall towers of Tridhos City Marina, stands a small, cream-coloured church with a tower. The latter bears the date 1912, the church 1910; another date, 1860, indicates when the first buildings on the site were erected. These early structures, belonging to the Presbyterian Mission, were the ones that brought solace to the

nervous Anna Leonowens when she sailed up the river one evening in 1862; and while the original ones have gone, along with the "forest of graceful boughs" around them, there is still a sense of timeless serenity about the old site.

Rather than rice, the godowns on the river are now more likely to hold tapioca (of which Thailand is one of the world's major producers); but otherwise the glimpses of crews unloading it sack by sack from barges, each worker receiving a chit from the foreman to verify the number of loads carried, can have changed little from those that greeted nineteenth-century sailors like Conrad.

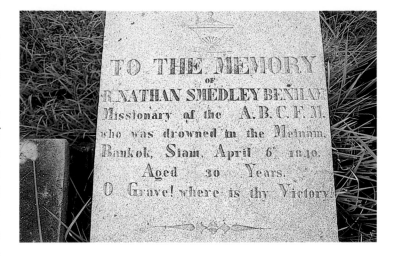

PREVIOUS PAGES:
*People resting at Wat
Mahathat, an impor-
tant centre of Buddhist
studies near the Grand
Palace; and an amulet
market near the temple.*

FACING PAGE: *The
Wang Lee House, built
by a Chinese immigrant
who made his fortune in
Bangkok.*

RIGHT: *A gravestone
for one of the many
nineteenth-century
foreigners who drowned
in the Chao Phraya.*

BELOW: *The Protestant
Cemetery, on land
granted to missionaries
by King Rama III.*

On the east bank, next to the Menam Hotel, is a little thicket of trees and shrubbery, through which the river sometimes pours at high tide. The old landing is no longer in use, so one must disembark elsewhere and enter from New Road to explore the Protestant Cemetery, established on a piece of land granted by King Rama IV. The place is not very well kept; weeds have taken over parts, and some of the gravestones are overturned; but a careful search reveals a remarkable cross-section of Bangkok's past. Dr Bradley lies here, along with his two wives and his daughter Irene; so do many of the eminent foreigners who worked as advisers to the Thai government; and numerous others, a few of them anonymous, carried away by the annual cholera epidemics or, in the case of some sailors, simply "drowned in the river".

On the same bank, further upstream near the Taksin Bridge, is a cluster of brightly gilded spires: Wat Yannawa, a temple dating from the early years of the city and popular with Chinese residents. It differs from others, however, in that one of its buildings is in the shape of a Chinese junk, with protective eyes on its prow and two stupas rising from its deck. This was an addition made by King Rama III, who took note of the fact that what

Bradley called "these monsters of the deep" were rapidly being rendered obsolete by the steamship and wanted future generations to remember the sort of vessel that played such a part in his capital's early growth.

East bank landmarks proliferate after this point, which also happens to be the centre of the most intensive modern development. Here one sees Assumption Cathedral, built in 1910 to replace another much older Roman Catholic church (which the Marquis de Beauvoir described in 1867 as "a modest building, very touching in its simplicity".); the handsome white facade of H.N. Andersen's East Asiatic Company, also erected in 1910 where the wooden buildings of his original company stood; at least a small part of the old Oriental Hotel, with its pediment crowned by a golden rising sun, and a garden extending to the river landing; the French embassy residence, near which the threatening gunboats tied up in 1893; and the old Customs House, sadly neglected nowadays but still managing to suggest a sense of its former importance in the kingdom's foreign trade.

The "trim, green, old-fashioned, and dignified British legation" that Maugham saw is gone—it was one of the first to leave the river, in the mid-

1920s, supposedly because the ambassador of the time was kept awake by a sawmill across the Chao Phraya—but the old Portuguese embassy is still in its original location and a neighbouring garden planted by the Royal Orchid Sheraton Hotel at least suggests the one where the first consul sat with his Baptist companions discussing the news of the day. A little further up is the Holy Rosary Church, which replaced the one built in 1787 on land granted to the Portuguese settlers by Rama I.

Across the river, between a group of old godowns, is the recently restored Wang Lee House, a reminder of the fortunes made by some of the hard-working Chinese who came to early Bangkok as humble labourers. Around 1850, Bishop Pallegoix estimated that the city's population numbered some 404,000, of whom half were Chinese, 120,000 were Thai, and the remainder were Cambodians, Peguans (Mons), Lao, Burmese, Malays, and Christians of various nationalities. Most Chinese were concentrated in the narrow streets of the area where Rama I moved their original community, but some who prospered built houses and temples on the west bank where land was more readily available.

More imagination is required to savour a few nearby sites. Just beyond the Memorial Bridge, for example, on the Thon Buri side, is where Robert Hunter's hospitable house stood; a cement jetty in the river is still a popular place for children to swim on late afternoons, and watching them it is not too difficult to summon up Hunter's amazement when he saw that strange creature with "two heads, four arms, and four legs" who turned out to be the Siamese twins.

Tha Tien, a landing on the opposite bank, is similarly mundane today, but assumes an added aura when one recalls that this is where foreign ambassadors and other official visitors disembarked on their way to audience with the king. Such occasions were often held at night, when it was cooler; Sir John Bowring was taken there at 8 p.m. and then "conveyed by eight bearers in an ornamented chair" to a series of stations before arriving at the palace.

Not far from Tha Tien, at least according to Neale, was a more sinister spot, one shunned by floating house owners in his time. The prince of an interior province (Neale says he was called "Peer-si-pi-foor, or some such hard name") had rashly rebelled, been defeated, and was brought to Bangkok for punishment. "The wretched criminal was condemned, first to have both his eyes put out by the application of searing irons, and then to be placed in an iron cage … which was suspended just so high above the waters of the river, that the unfortunate captive by stretching his arms through the close iron bars could barely manage to touch the ripple of the waters with the extreme tip of his fingers." After three days and nights he died of thirst, but the spectacle had sufficiently intimidated river dwellers so that none would live there.

Still a prominent feature on the west bank is Santa Cruz Church, heart of the former "Settlement of the Holy Cross", where descendants of Ayutthaya's Portuguese community gathered in the new capital. The first church, however, was a small one, later rebuilt in 1834 by Bishop Pallegoix; the present edifice dates from 1913. A little further, to the right of the mouth of Klong Bangkok Yai, are the restored walls of Vichai Prasit Fortress, on the site of the one built by the French in the late Ayutthaya period, where now purely decorative cannons still command the river front.

Equally familiar to every early visitor was the towering, porcelain-encrusted *prang* of Wat Arun, the Temple of Dawn, though most of them

FOLLOWING PAGES: Chinese-style guardian figure at Wat Arun, the Temple of Dawn; a detail of the porcelain mosaic that decorates the temple; and sunset over Wat Arun. The central prang was completed during the reign of Rama III.

A Chao Phraya discovery

Late one afternoon in 1824, as the Scottish trader Robert Hunter was returning to his house on the west bank of the Chao Phraya, he was struck by an extraordinary sight before him in the water. "It was a creature that appeared to have two heads, four arms, and four legs," Dr Dan Bradley later recorded, "all of which were moving in perfect harmony. As Mr Hunter watched, the object climbed into a nearby boat, and to his amazement he realised that he had been looking at two small boys who were joined together at the waist."

Chang and Eng, as the boys were named, were then thirteen years old, the sons of a half-Chinese, half-Malay mother and a Chinese father. They were not the first conjoined twins—two sisters, joined at the hips and shoulders, were born in 1100 at Biddenden, Kent, and became known as the Biddenden Maids—but they certainly became the most celebrated. With Hunter's assistance, they left Bangkok in 1826 aboard an American ship and shortly after their arrival in Boston they were on display as "The Siamese Double Boys", which soon became "The Siamese Twins".

They never returned to their homeland. After years of successful touring in America and Europe—many under the shrewd sponsorship of Phineas T. Barnum—they tired of notoriety, became naturalised American citizens (with the surname of Bunker), and, in 1839, settled as farmers in a small North Carolina town. There, despite considerable local opposition, they courted and married two sisters, Sarah and Adelaide Yates. Chang and Adelaide had three boys and seven girls, while Eng and Sarah had seven boys and five girls, all normal. Because of the size of their families, they eventually had to live in separate houses, spending three days in each.

Chang and Eng entered show business once more, to recoup some of the serious financial losses they suffered during the American Civil War, but finally returned to North Carolina for good in 1871. Three years later Chang died in his sleep of severe bronchitis; Eng died a few hours later, possibly of fear. A post-mortem revealed that it would have been impossible to separate the twins during their lifetime.

In the 1960s, according to a biography written by a relative of Robert Hunter's, there were an estimated thousand descendants of the twins then living in the United States, all of them physically normal.

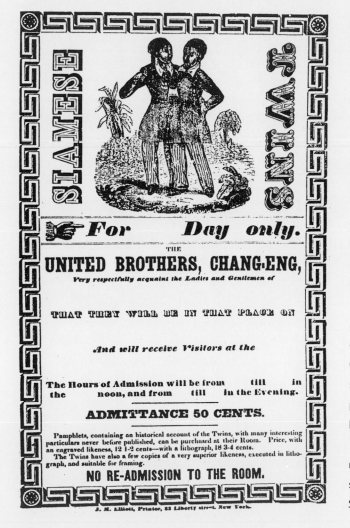

called it Wat Chang, the "Elephant Temple". In another form, it was there when King Taksin made Thon Buri his capital and served as the royal chapel for his nearby palace. The great central *prang* was started by Rama II but due to technical problems of building on the wet river-bank it did not reach its present elevation of 81 metres until the next reign. The temple was the main destination for the splendid royal barge processions that were an annual spectacle, and the Chao Phraya views it offers have proved irresistible to countless photographers ever since the first camera appeared in the kingdom.

The river bends just above Wat Arun, and from behind a group of nondescript modern buildings on the opposite bank the Grand Palace enclosure comes suddenly, dramatically into view. No imagination is needed here, no association with long-ago events and characters: this peerless panorama of golden spires and rounded Khmer-style *prangs* dominates the river as memorably as ever, glittering with a romance undimmed by the passage of two centuries. More than any other single sight in Thailand, it links past and present effortlessly; and particularly at night, when the buildings are illuminated, it invests the Chao Phraya with an aura of pure magic.

There are other places, too, where one can recapture some of Bangkok's old riverine allure. Yet perhaps the greatest revelation provided by a trip along the Chao Phraya today comes less from its past than from a growing awareness of its contemporary role. Heavily loaded barges still move in long, stately processions past the high-rise buildings, towed by puffing little tugboats, and if they are now more often made of steel than teak, their contents are no less essential. Foreign ships still bring most of Thailand's imports to the sprawling Port of Bangkok (over 10 million metric tons in 1992) and carry out most of its exports (more than 8.0 million tons). Crowded ferries still go up and down throughout the day, long-tailed motor boats cluster around landings to collect passengers, and riverside restaurants beckon after nightfall with festive strings of coloured lights.

The Chao Phraya, one realises with a sense of discovery, remains a vital waterway—not so pervasive a presence as it once was, perhaps, but still a significant part of Bangkok's everyday life.

PREVIOUS PAGES: *The skyline of central Bangkok, seen across the river from Thon Buri; sightseers take a picture on Phra Pinklao Bridge.*

LEFT: *Tridhos City Marina with the Krung Thep Bridge in the foreground; and the Rama IX Bridge, opened to commemorate H.M. the King's sixtieth birthday.*

FACING PAGE: *Varied styles of contemporary architecture along the river.*

Modern architecture along the river

LEFT: *The Port of Bangkok at Klong Toey, still the main entry point for most imported goods.*

ABOVE: *Repairing a freighter in the river.*

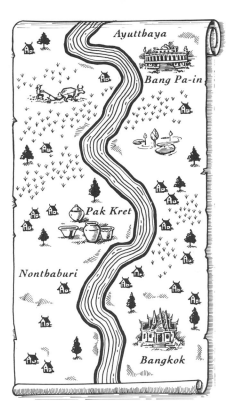

BANGKOK TO AYUTTHAYA

Betwixt Bangkok and Siam [Ayutthaya], you meet with a great many Aldees or Villages, that almost everywhere border the River. These villages are no more than a great many Huts or Hovels raised upon high Pillars, because of the Inundation. They are made of Bambous, which is a Tree whose Timber is much used in that Country. … Near the Villages are the Bazaars or floating Market-places, where the Siamese, who go up and down the River, find their Victuals ready dressed; that's to say, Fruit, boiled Rice, Rack (which is a kind of Strong Water made of Rice and Lime) and some Ragouts after the Siamese Mode, which a Frenchman could not taste."

In 1685, when Father Guy Tachard wrote this description, the Chao Phraya was one of the busiest river roads in Asia, particularly the final stretch leading to the great city of Ayutthaya. The traffic, of course, declined greatly after Ayutthaya's fall, but many of the villages could still be seen strung out along the banks during the nineteenth and early twentieth centuries; the famous Thai poet Sunthorn Phu, who travelled upstream in 1808, mentions half a dozen that he saw from his boat, as well as numerous market gardens and fruit orchards.

The largest settlement near Bangkok was one popularly known as Talat Khwan, officially Muang Non and today Nonthaburi, which appears on seventeenth-century European maps as Talacouan or Talatquan. Most accounts of the early Bangkok period describe this as a bustling community where silk and fruit were sold from a long row of shops on bamboo rafts moored near the shore; in 1834, Bishop Pallegoix estimated that there were about 500 houses, from which he deduced that the population was around 5,000. Afterwards, as far as Pak Kret, the banks were thick with trees and lacy clumps of bamboo out of which rose the layered roofs of Buddhist temples.

At the end of the rainy season, before dams and irrigation canals had brought a degree of flood control to the lower delta, Nonthaburi was transformed into a vast lake by water flowing down the Chao Phraya. The French naturalist and explorer Henri Mouhot, heading up-river in October of 1858, wrote in his diary, "The current runs very strongly at this season, and it took us five days to get about seventy miles. At night we suffered dreadfully from the mosquitoes, and even during the day had

to keep up the incessant fanning to drive off these pestilent little vampires. They were so numerous that you could catch them by handfuls, and their humming resembled that of a hive of bees. … As the country was entirely inundated, we could not land anywhere, and even after killing a bird I frequently could not get at it. All this was very tantalising, for the banks of the stream are very gay and attractive, nature wearing here her richest dress."

Today the villages are barely discernible

amid the sizeable buildings and elegant houses of suburbs that extend for many kilometres, among the most visible being the towers of a huge housing project that rises somewhat improbably from the flat fields of Nonthaburi and that bears the impressive name of Muang Ek, literally "town of the first rank". (In the past *muang*, or towns, were divided into four ranks, *ek* being the highest; the developers of Muang Ek have thus displayed a sense of history as well as shrewd advertising in their choice of a name for the project.)

One spectacle that would have intrigued early travellers even more is the sight of planes passing over on their way into Don Muang, established in 1914 and the oldest major airport in the world still being used in its original location. The site was chosen by Prince Chakrabongse, Chief of the Army General Staff, because it was on slightly higher ground than the capital and thus less subject to seasonal floods; no road then connected it with the city, the only access being by railway or by the Chao Phraya. Some of the early international airlines operated flying boats and actually landed on the river and moored at a terminal in Nonthaburi, from which passengers were ferried down to such hotels as the Oriental.

Despite modern developments like Muang Ek, this part of the river is still bordered by rice fields, with long irrigation canals dividing them into an intricate chequer-board pattern that many assume to have been a feature of the landscape for as long as there have been settlements along the Chao Phraya. In fact, rice did not become a major Thai export until the second half of the nineteenth century after treaties were signed with various Western countries that created a growing demand; and it was only during the reign of King Chulalongkorn that canals were dug specifically to open the lands

Potters of Ko Kret

Among the traditional skills brought by Mon refugees who settled on the river island of Ko Kret in the eighteenth century was pottery making, and this continues to provide an income for many of their ancestors today.

About ten kilns can be seen along the shady pathways that meander around the quiet, picturesque island, still free of motor cars since no bridge yet joins it to the mainland. Mostly they produce simple, utilitarian flower pots, made to order for dealers and nursery owners in Bangkok, though at least one turns out more elaborate Mon-style creations such as decorated water jars and lightly glazed cooking pots similar to those found in ancient Ayutthaya and popular with visitors who travel to Ko Kret on holiday excursions.

The clay now used comes mostly from Pathum Thani, another Mon settlement further up the river. It is mixed with sand and squeezed through a machine to form long, log-like lengths. These are cut into shorter lengths, depending on the size of the pot desired, and deftly shaped on a wheel before being baked for two or three hours in primitive kilns fired with dried coconut-palm fronds. Each worker can produce about 300 pots a day. The completed products are then taken to the mainland by boat and loaded on to lorries for delivery.

Although few of the ultimate buyers realise it, the potters of Ko Kret provide a rare link with a past that is vanishing along much of the modern Chao Phraya.

FACING PAGE: *A potter on Ko Kret shaping clay on a wheel.*
ABOVE: *Kiln being fired with palm-leaf fuel.*
RIGHT: *Mon-style pottery, made by one of the Ko Kret kilns and exhibited in a museum on the island.*

LEFT: *A saleswoman in a Ko Kret pottery shop; flower pots stacked beneath one of the houses.*
FACING PAGE: *Drying newly made pots in the sun; and storing pots before delivery to buyers in Bangkok.*

THESE PAGES: *A grin from a boy paddling his boat; another lad climbs the rudder of an unladen barge.*

vista of the broad river in all its moods: as it glittered in the sun, or reflected the many-coloured twilight, or turned quiet and mysterious under the stars. But perhaps the best thing evoked by the name Bang Pa-in had to do with the expectant holiday spirit, the getting away from old routines, the relaxed protocol, the carefree atmosphere. Bang Pa-in, to put it briefly, meant *sanuk, tuenten* … meant fun and excitement."

The thoughts are those of the heroine of Kukrit Pramoj's famous novel *Si Phaendin* (Four Reigns) and sum up the reactions among the royal ladies residing in the Grand Palace during the reign of King Chulalongkorn whenever such an outing was proposed.

Although most of the present buildings date from that time, Bang Pa-in was also popular in the seventeenth century, with Ayutthayan kings who found it an equally pleasant and convenient respite from the rigid formality of palace life. After the fall of Ayutthaya, it was abandoned for close to a century and then given a new life by King Mongkut (Rama IV), who built a few rustic structures and often stopped there on his trips to visit the ruins of the old capital.

Under King Chulalongkorn, excursions to Bang Pa-in became a regular part of the Court's routine, particularly in the cool dry season, and many improvements were made to the place. An anonymous Englishman who wrote an account of his stay in Thailand offered the following description, rather less than enthusiastic, of the summer palace in 1890:

"Bang Pa-in consists of two islands; on the one is the palace of the King, and on the other a Buddhist church in the Gothic style, with stained windows, pews, and altar complete. On the island now occupied by the palace there originally stood a

"BANG PA-IN! At that period, to most Palace people in Bangkok, Bang Pa-in was something of a magical word. Even if you had never been there yourself the mention of its name conjured up visions of the greenest of green countryside to gladden your city heart and soul. Here the heat occasionally could be oppressive, but over there you would have the pure, fresh, cooling breeze all day long. Already in your mind's eye you could see the rice-fields gently waving, stretching away to the horizon. You could see those fairy-land lotus ponds with their pink and white blooms and drink in the

humble building which the late King [Rama IV] called his 'shooting-box'. He was very much attached to the spot, planted it out with mango-trees, and escaped when he could to this peaceful spot for rest from the cares of State. The present King, out of reverence for all that his father loved, adopted the place for his holiday-making. A summer palace was run up and European contractors made fortunes. A taste for everything foreign came into vogue about that time, and instead of Siamese architects, foreigners were invited to submit their plans, and they were accepted. No graceful pagodas are to be seen, but houses fancifully and slightly built, round towers, chimneys of gas-works never completed, and the spire of a Gothic church which shoots up into the sky. In the midst of all one gem of native architecture rears its graceful head, but it occupies a humble position, and is quite overshadowed by its European rivals."

The description is not quite accurate, for there is in fact an old Ayutthaya-period temple called Wat Chumpon Nikayaram near the palace, dating from the early seventeenth century. Moreover, the varied architectural styles, alien though they certainly are, have a definite charm reminiscent of a Victorian theme park, which in Bang Pa-in's heyday made the eighty-kilometre boat trip up the Chao Phraya an eagerly anticipated event. On one such excursion, in 1883, the high spirits turned to sorrow as a result of an ancient law dealing with the rescue from water of royal personages.

The historian Quaritch Wales gives this free translation of the law in question: "If the royal barge founders, the boatmen must swim away: if they remain near they are to be executed. If the boat founders and the royal person falls into the water and is about to drown, let the boatmen stretch out the signal-spear and throw coconuts so that he may grasp them if he can. If he cannot they may let him grasp the signal-spear. If they lay hold of him to rescue him they are to be executed. He who throws the coconuts is to be rewarded with 40 ticals of silver and one gold basin. If the barge sinks and someone else sees the coconuts thrown and goes to save the royal person, the punishment is double and his family is to be killed. If the barge founders and someone throws the coconuts so that they float toward the shore (i.e. away from the royal person) his throat is to be cut and his home confiscated."

It was supposedly because of this law that King Chulalongkorn's much-beloved Queen Sunanta and her unborn child were drowned when

LEFT: *A small boat launched as an offering near Wat Prawan Ruatom, where the boat in which Queen Sunanta tragically drowned is kept as a shrine.*

the boat in which she was being towed by a launch overturned as it was nearing Bang Pa-in. Some farmers on the shore could have saved her, according to Dr Malcolm Smith, "but were forbidden to do so by an official who said it was against the law. And so she drowned, the victim of Red Tape. The antiquated law was remembered, but in modernising the transport they had forgotten the coconuts."

The king was heartbroken and erected an elaborate monument to the queen's memory at the summer palace, bearing inscriptions in both Thai and English. The boat in which she was riding is still on display as an object of veneration at a temple on the river, draped with floral offerings brought by villagers living nearby.

After King Chulalongkorn's death, his principal consort, Queen Saovabha, went into retirement with her large retinue of attendants at Phra Thai Palace in Bangkok. One of the few customs

she continued, however, was the annual visit to Bang Pa-in. "She travelled there by water," Dr Smith wrote in his memoirs of life as a royal physician, "and with a canal at the very gates of [her palace] this was an easy matter. One of the great house-boats that had been used for picnic tours in the past was taken from its shelter and cleaned and polished and made ready for the trip. Like some old friend returning to greet her after long absence it drew up at her landing, shining and resplendent as it had been in the days when she was a young and active woman. Only one thing was missing. The gondoliers in their scarlet costumes were missing. Their place had been taken by the steam launch and tow rope, a swifter and smoother means of transport. The journey that would have required two days before could now be made in a few hours. …

"While the Queen was in residence at Bang Pa-in Palace it was a busy place. Something of the

RIGHT: *Western-style reception hall at Bang Pa-in, a popular gathering place for the court of King Rama V.*

gaiety it had known in the days of King Chulalongkorn was recaptured. Parties went up by launch and train—not to see the Queen, there was no hope of that for she never left her room—but to meet their acquaintances, to see the shows, to have a picnic. To all her friends and relatives she kept open house, and they came and went as they pleased. Troops of dancers were sent up from Bangkok to perform, theatrical shows were arranged. They took place out of doors. Under a moon riding high in a cloudless sky it was a picturesque sight. The stage was set up on one side of a large lawn and some rows of chairs were placed in front of it, but they were not much used. The audience for the most part preferred to sit on the ground or stand about. Some came to watch for a bit; others found it a convenient place for conversation; some as the night wore on fell asleep. No one ever thought of seeing a performance through."

Such diversions ended with the queen's death in 1919, and Bang Pa-in, while never abandoned as it was after the fall of Ayutthaya, fell into general disuse. It came to life again in the present reign, most memorably one evening during the Bangkok bicentenary celebrations in 1982 when it was the scene of a gala event. Once more the lamps were lit, music wafted through the trees, and guests in formal dress strolled along the winding walkways, past the ornamental European statues, the Italian-style palace and the exquisite little Thai pavilion reflected in the waters of a lake, the beautiful water gates through which royal barges once arrived, the splendid Chinese Hall (made in China and sent in pieces for reassembly at the site), the neo-Gothic observatory. For those fortunate enough to be there, past and present merged for a magical moment and it was easy to understand Bang Pa-in's potent appeal.

Barge life along the river

PREVIOUS PAGES AND THESE PAGES: *Views of barge life along the Chao Phraya; many families live almost full-time on such barges, which ply the river between Ayutthaya and Bangkok.*

FOLLOWING PAGES: *Dredging the river for sand, which will then be carried down to Bangkok for use in construction and as land fill; a ruined stupa from the Ayutthaya period.*

THE CHAO PHRAYA is a broad stream as it approaches the old capital, with huge floating masses of water hyacinth, a number of sizeable islands, and sandbars that presented a threat to trade ships en route to Ayutthaya. Near one of the islands, Ko Phra, travellers such as Sunthorn Phu could still see the mast of a Chinese junk which had sunk a century earlier. Prominent today are enormous orange and blue dredgers permanently placed in the river to extract sand, which is loaded on to barges and taken to Bangkok for the construction industry.

In 1968, according to a newspaper report, when an independent dredger identified only as Mr Snoh was working near the island of Ko Rian, he brought up a large anchor from the bottom. He regarded it as valuable scrap and placed it in his barge for eventual sale in Bangkok. The night before he was to leave for the capital, however, a most peculiar thing occurred: above the place where the anchor was stored, he and his family saw a bright flickering flame which then disappeared, leaving no sign of a fire behind. Mr Snoh and his family were then afflicted by such severe headaches that they had to delay their departure; during the night a young woman appeared to him in a dream and ordered him to place the anchor beneath a sacred bodhi tree at Wat Phananchoeng, an old temple just outside Ayutthaya, particularly popular with local Chinese.

This was done the next day, and mediums were later called to investigate the mysterious object. They pronounced that it had been part of a junk bringing a Chinese princess named Soi Dok Mai, who popular legend claimed was on her way to marry a Thai prince; she drowned in the accident and the prince, grief-stricken, killed himself.

It should perhaps be noted that another legend claims Soi Dok Mai committed suicide when a king she had come to marry in 1326, before the actual founding of Ayutthaya, failed to pay her proper respect; according to this version, she was cremated at Wat Phananchoeng and an immense Buddha image was erected by the king in her memory. In any event, both the anchor and the image are still enshrined at the temple and still kept regularly supplied with offerings by believers.

Not far above Bang Pa-in, the traveller today sees a half-ruined spire rising from a mass of greenery on the river bank. It is the first suggestion of far more spectacular examples that lie just ahead, the haunting remains of what was once the largest and most splendid capital in the region.

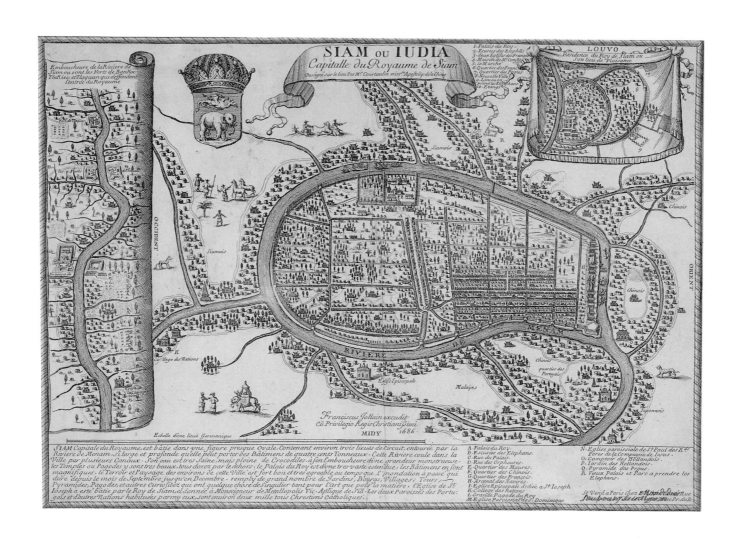

PREVIOUS PAGES:
A reclining Buddha image at Wat Buddhaisawan in Ayutthaya.

FACING PAGE: *A seventeenth-century map of Ayutthaya, which ruled Thailand for 400 years.*
RIGHT: *Engraving of barges in Ayutthaya at the time of the French embassies toward the end of the seventeenth century.*

AYUTTHAYA

"In the Kingdom of Siam where I was on two occasions, I went to the city of Ayutthaya where the court of the King can be found, and I can state it is the greatest affair I saw in all those parts. This city is like Venice because one travels more by water than one does by land. I heard it be said by many that there were over two hundred thousand boats, both large and small. I do not know if there are two hundred thousand boats but I did see a league's length of waterways which was so full that one could not pass; for many fairs are held on the rivers round the city and these are like the feasts of the idols. And to each one of these fairs come five hundred boats and at times over one thousand."

Written in the mid-sixteenth century by Fernao Mendes Pinto—soldier, merchant, traveller, and later Jesuit missionary—this is one of the earliest European impressions of Ayutthaya, then almost halfway through its 400-year rule. Ahead lay times of even greater splendour, when it became perhaps the leading centre of trade in the region, and also a time of decline, defeat, and almost total destruction. Today it is a city of ruins large and small, impressive and barely discernible, all telling tales of the past.

Ayutthaya was founded by a prince of U-Thong, who later ruled under the name of Ramathibodi. According to a version of the Ayutthaya Royal Chronicles quoted by David K. Wyatt in his history of Thailand, the prince was seeking a place free from the scourge of smallpox and marched with his men "until they came to a large river and saw a circular island, smooth, level, and apparently clean, standing in the centre of the area. … In 712, a Year of the Tiger, second of the decade, on Friday, the sixth day of the waxing moon of the fifth month, at three *nalika* and nine *bat* after the break of dawn [i.e., Friday, 4 March 1351, shortly after nine o'clock in the morning], the Capital City of Ayutthaya was first established."

Actually, the island had been created by digging a canal through the neck of a peninsula at a point where the Pasak and Lop Buri rivers joined the Chao Phraya, and some sources claim it was already a busy trading centre at the time Prince U-Thong decided to found his capital there; Wat Phananchoeng, where the Chao Phraya curved to

the left, had been built in 1326 and was an important centre of worship. The site was ideally situated for a major city, however, not only from the standpoint of defence but also from that of future trade. Produce coming by water from both north and east had to pass through it, and the route to the sea was both broad and navigable. Moreover, it stood at the junction of the old and new Chao Phraya deltas, high enough to remain dry when the lands below were completely inundated.

Simple mud walls were constructed at first around the island, but these were soon replaced with more impressive fortifications as the city's power grew, punctuated with water gates that allowed entry to the canals. Nicholas Gervaise, who saw it toward the end of the seventeenth century, described it as "a most attractive island, which is approximately seven leagues in circumference. The enclosure of the city is only about two leagues, and this includes the royal palace. ... The great river flows under the walls of the southern, eastern, and western sides and through the city in three main branches, which traverse it from end to end, thus making it into another Venice. It might even be claimed that its position is finer than that of Venice,

even though the buildings are less magnificent, for the canals which are formed by the branches of the river are very long, very straight, and deep enough to carry the largest vessels. The city is divided by quarters and by streets as in Europe; the Europeans call these quarters camps and the Siamese call them *ban* [i.e. villages]. The King's quarter is the finest, because of the great squares and the pagodas which surround it."

In a reconstruction of the capital at its peak, based on old maps, descriptions, and aerial photographs, the architect Sumet Jumsai has found that the city walls, excluding those of the palace area, extended for some twelve kilometres and had seventeen forts. There were more than ninety city gates and twenty-two more for the Grand Palace, about twenty of which were water gates; canals within the city totalled fifty-six kilometres in length, spanned by numerous bridges.

The wealth of Ayutthaya was based on trade with the outside world, somewhat surprisingly in view of the fact that, as the historian Charnvit Kasetsart has noted, it was "a mere hinterland kingdom with the majority of its population not skilled in sea-faring activities." This difficulty was overcome by enlisting the services of outsiders, particularly the Chinese with whom the early Ayutthayan kings maintained a traditional tribute-trade system. The first Ming envoy came to Ayutthaya in 1369, the same year King Ramathibodi died; under the third king, Baromracha I, no less than eight Siamese missions were sent to China, carrying such unusual local offerings as elephants and six-legged turtles and receiving in return silks and satin. Overseas Chinese trading communities on the Gulf of Thailand also contributed to the kingdom's prosperity, exporting large quantities of sappanwood (used to produce dye), eagle wood,

animal hides, pepper, ivory, and various other native products.

Indian traders later appeared on the Chao Phraya, bringing goods that had crossed the Bay of Bengal and been unloaded at Mergui, then carried across the peninsula by river and overland to other ships waiting at Prachuab on the gulf.

Enriched by such trade, as well as by a growing empire that eventually covered most of present-day Thailand and parts of neighbouring Cambodia, Laos, and Malaysia, Ayutthaya's physical splendour also increased, with over 500 magnificent Buddhist temples, three royal palaces, and a number of public buildings, most of which were erected during the first two centuries of its rule. The kings, with a few notable exceptions, became distant, god-like figures, surrounded by Brahmin-inspired ritual. Englebert Kaempfer, arriving at the Dutch factory, or trading post, one morning in 1690 learned that "the Director of our factory had notice given him, to keep his people within the doors the next morning, because His Majesty intended to go

abroad. When the King of Siam goes abroad, everybody must keep out of the way, as they do in Persia when the King's women go out. All the windows are shut, and not the least noise to be heard."

The first European to arrive, in 1511, was a Portuguese named Duarte Fernandez, sent by the commander of a force that had just conquered Malacca, over which Ayutthaya claimed vague rights. Fernandez came up the Chao Phraya on a Chinese junk and made a favourable impression on the reigning king, possibly assisted by the fact that he spoke a little Thai and presented to the king a sword with a gold scabbard encrusted with diamonds. A Thai envoy returned with him to Malacca, also bearing gifts, and within a year a Portuguese agent was established in Ayutthaya; in 1516, the first treaty was concluded between Siam and a European power.

The Portuguese became a familiar presence, one that lasted throughout the Ayutthaya period and also well into early Bangkok. Besides trading, they gave instruction in European weapons, took part in wars as mercenaries, and built Roman Catholic churches outside the city walls. They also intermarried freely with local women and produced numerous offspring. "The result," as E.W. Hutchinson observed, "has been a greater increase in the Christian population of these eastern lands than would have occurred otherwise, but it has produced a population which, as time went on, retained little that was Portuguese except its high-sounding names."

In the early seventeenth century, following a brief period during which Ayutthaya became a vassal of Burma, the number of resident foreigners increased. Among them was a colony of Japanese, some of them Catholic converts fleeing persecution in their own country, and others adventurers,

NEAR RIGHT: *The feet of a reclining Buddha image;* stone *singhas, or royal lions.*

FAR RIGHT: *A Buddha head, wrapped in the twisting roots of a bodhi tree.*

FOLLOWING PAGES: *Headless images at Wat Chai Wattanaram.*

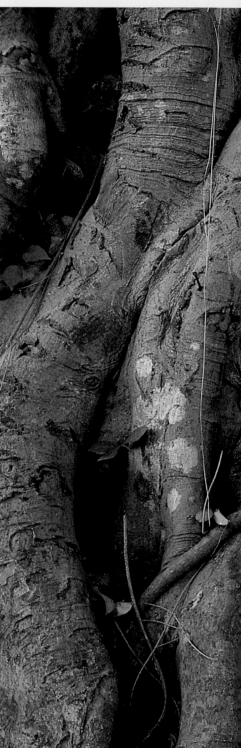

AMONG THE many tragic consequences of the virtual destruction of Ayutthaya in 1767 was the loss of nearly all its historical records. Much of our present knowledge of the capital, both of its physical appearance and its daily life, is thus drawn from foreign sources, specifically from the journals or later accounts written by a relatively small group who spent varying periods of time there.

FACING PAGE: Remains of Constantine Phaulkon's palace at Lop Buri, which also served as a residence for foreign ambassadors.

The early traders and mercenaries were not literary men—some, indeed, were barely literate—and few recorded their impressions. Of these, some were plainly coloured by imagination, like those of a certain Captain Erwin, otherwise unidentified, who happened to meet the famous diarist Samuel Pepys in London in 1666. "The King of Siam seldom goes out without thirty or forty thousand people with him," Pepys recorded, "and not a word spoke nor a hum or cough in the whole company to be heard. [Erwin] tells me the punishment frequently there for malefactors is cutting off the crown of the head, which they do very dextrously, leaving the brains bare, which kills them presently."

By far the greatest number of accounts, and the most reliable, come from a brief period near the end of the seventeenth century, which also happened to be the peak of Ayutthaya's power and prosperity. Of the cast of notable characters involved, two in particular stand out, for without them and their strange involvement with one another, the others would not have come.

One was King Narai, a somewhat anachronistic figure who came to the throne in 1656 and who managed to combine the qualities of an all-powerful, semi-divine monarch with an exceptional degree of tolerance and a strong curiosity about the outside world. The other was a sharp-witted Greek named Constantine Phaulkon ("Monsieur Constance" in many contemporary accounts) who appeared at the same time on the Ayutthaya scene.

A controversial figure during his brief moment of glory, Phaulkon remains one today; but in the complex, often impenetrable world of Thai politics he was a recognisable type to the Europeans of Ayutthaya, and this perhaps also explains why he has captivated so many Western writers over the years. "One of the most amazing of the adventurers who have made the East the scene of their exploits," observed Somerset Maugham, who in the 1920s made a special detour to visit the ruins of Phaulkon's palace at Lop Buri, where King Narai often retreated for pleasure. In *Siamese White*, the story of an English freebooter named Samuel White, Maurice Collis summarises Phaulkon as "one of those rare and fascinating youths who mature early and by their brilliance, industry, and charm captivate all who meet them. Though of formidable genius, such persons do not at first alarm, for they can combine usefulness with servility, but when their talents and guile have lifted them into power they arouse a terrified loathing in the hearts of their opponents."

One more character analysis might be useful, this from a man who wrote out of direct experience. The Chevalier de Forbin was a French naval officer who modernised the forts at Bangkok in 1686 and rendered other services to Phaulkon and King Narai. He had good reason to be wary of the Greek; indeed, he suspected Phaulkon of trying to poison him to prevent his returning to France with unflattering revelations about affairs in Ayutthaya; yet he was able to see two sides to the man:

"He had high and noble aspirations: his capacity was above the average. No plan was too great for him to guide it to a successful conclusion with wisdom and circumspection. He would indeed have been fortunate if these qualities had not been marred by the most conspicuous defects, of which the chief were boundless ambition, insatiable and often sordid avarice, a jealousy which took offence at trifles and led him to be hard, cruel, and devoid of both pity and honesty."

The object of these (and many more) attempts at evaluation was born in obscurity on the island of Cephalonia, then under Venetian rule, in 1647. While still a boy, perhaps ten or twelve, he went to sea aboard an English merchant ship. The next few years were spent on various ships, never rising very high in rank but gaining varied experiences in both European and Eastern waters; he was eventually employed by the British East India Company and, through friends made there, became a private trader. After being shipwrecked on the coast of southern Thailand, he arrived in Ayutthaya in 1678, unknown and powerless.

He had important assets, however: he was energetic, fluent in a number of languages, and experienced in international trade, and he undoubtedly possessed considerable charm as well as a natural talent for politics. These led to his appointment as interpreter for the powerful Barcalon, the official in charge of King Narai's trade, and soon carried him to such heights that by the time of the Chevalier de Forbin's arrival he was a confidant of the king with the title of Phra Vichayen and had splendid palaces at Ayutthaya and Lop Buri, a retinue of servants, and a beautiful part-Japanese wife renowned for her culinary skills. This woman, whom he married at the Portuguese church in 1682, was a descendant of the Japanese Catholics who had taken refuge in Ayutthaya, and to marry her Phaulkon returned to the faith into which he had been born but from which he had strayed in his wanderings.

This is important, for he was brought back to the church by French Jesuit priests who had

LEFT: *Engraving from 1686, showing King Narai on one of his royal elephants.*
FACING PAGE: *King Narai's Lop Buri palace; and a Khmer-style deity, now displayed in the palace precincts.*

come to Siam some years earlier, and it was at least partly due to their influence that he embarked on the grandiose schemes that would cost him both his power and his life. The motives that lay behind his efforts to forge an alliance between Narai's kingdom and the France of Louis XIV are tangled, however, and would require much more space to explore in detail. Did he really believe, for example, as many of his Jesuit friends certainly did, that the king (and, by extension, all of the country) was ripe for conversion to Christianity? Or was it a shrewd political move to counter-balance growing English and Dutch influence in the region? Or was he, as most of the resident English believed, merely doing it out of an innate love of intrigue and a desire to line his own pockets?

Whatever the reasons, King Narai decided to send three ambassadors to France. They left Ayutthaya aboard a French vessel, the *Soleil d'Orient*, in 1680, carrying not only the envoys but interpret-

Songs of the river

The dazzling processions of gilded barges and other noble craft on the Chao Phraya appealed both to eye and ear. As Khunying Chamnongsri Rutnin and Tipsuda Sundaravej have written, "Since the barges were manned by large crews, necessity arose for the coordination of the movements of the crewsmen. To serve this purpose and to uplift the spirit of the men, rhythmic barge songs were chanted. Verses used for this purpose are known as *bot he rua*, which in themselves have become a poetic literary genre. Different verse forms are used to give varying rhythms to fit the different speeds of the strokes and patterns of movement of the paddles."

Bot he rua written for ceremonial occasions were formal and serious, while others were less restricted and commonly had nothing at all to do with boats. The crew that brought Sir John Bowring to Bangkok in 1855 sang, "Row, row, I smell the rice," in anticipation of the meal that waited for them.

A barge song that survives from Ayutthaya was written by the eldest son of King Baromakot, who reigned toward the end of the period, and describes the royal craft:

When the King journeys on water
He graces the jewelled throne
Amid his magnificent entourage
Of golden barges in proud procession...
Barges shaped like mighty beasts
Throng the sovereign fleet
Attendant barges with flying banners
Stir the turbulent tide

Another royal *bot he rua* composer was King Rama II of Bangkok. His song describes the delicacies prepared by a young princess who would later become his queen:

Steamy nest of swallow
Warm and mellow to the taste
Seeing the nest without a bird
I hunger for my lover's nest...
Ruby red pomegranates
Adorn the plate like jewels
My love wears a ruby ring
With alluring red sparkles

And for a final example, this is from the gifted pen of King Rama VI, offering a glimpse of the new capital that was then taking shape:

Shadows of mountains,
Created by the evening sun,
Bring back memories
Of the great city to my vision.
Tiered buildings line the roads,
Marked by streetlamps so bright,
As brilliant as they would be
In full and glaring daylight.
Townsmen sport their motorcars.
Women, colourfully dressed,
Show off the newest styles,
Hoping the men would be impressed.

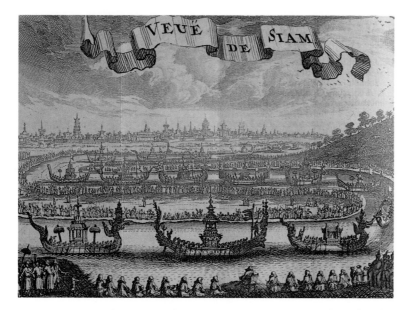

ABOVE: *A seventeenth-
century engraving
showing the barge
procession that brought
a letter from Louis XIV
to King Narai.*

FOLLOWING PAGE:
*Engraving shows King
Narai leaning out of his
window to receive the
letter from Louis XIV.*

the king, who knew all about his past, declined to do so. Such was the Abbé's charm, however, that he did succeed in getting himself appointed as deputy to Chaumont.

A third member of the embassy who deserves mention was Father Tachard, a Jesuit who quickly became intimate with Phaulkon and even served, for a time, as his secretary. Tachard was a schemer—the "bad character" in the story, according to historian Dirk Van der Cruyse—who plotted behind the ambassador's back and advocated French military involvement in Ayutthaya. Choisy would later write bitterly, "Chaumont and myself were but theatrical performers; the good Father was the real ambassador, in charge of the secret negotiations."

Despite the frustrations, Choisy enjoyed his stay in cosmopolitan Ayutthaya, as the vivid account he wrote makes clear. "We went for an excursion outside the town," he recounted. "I am never tired of admiring this very large city on an island surrounded by a river three times bigger than the Seine, full of French, English, Dutch, Chinese, Japanese, and Siamese vessels and an uncountable number of barges, and gilded galleys with sixty oarsmen. The King is beginning to build ships in the

European manner; three have recently been launched on to the waters. But something still more admirable is that on both sides of this island are the quarters or villages inhabited by the different nationalities; all the wooden houses are in the water, the buffaloes, cows, and pigs in the air [i.e., on raised floors]. The streets are alleys of fresh flowing water as far as the eye can see, under huge green trees, and in these tiny houses there is a great crowd of people. Slightly beyond the villages are the broad landscapes of rice which one passes through by boat. The rice is always above the water; and the horizon is limited by big trees, above which one sees here and there the shining towers and pyramids of the pagodas covered with two or three layers of gilding. I do not know if I am presenting your imagination an attractive view, but certainly I have never seen anything finer, though with the exception of the pagodas everything is still of natural simplicity."

The visit contained at least one moment of high comedy, according to Choisy's account. Shortly after their arrival the all-important ceremony to present Louis XIV's letter to King Narai took place in the royal palace. Phaulkon had explained that Thai kings did not accept letters from the hands of ambassadors, no matter how grand, and suggested that the document be placed in a cup at the end of a long stick and thereby lifted up to the throne. Chaumont refused, saying that either the throne must be lowered or he must be provided with a platform from which he could personally deliver it; and "Mr Constance" finally agreed, with what one suspects was some exasperation.

"However, when we entered the room, we saw the King at a window at least six feet high. The Ambassador muttered to me, 'I cannot give him the letter at the end of a stick, and I shall never do it.' I

build a dais, and had resolved, in case the Ambassador did not raise the letter to the height of his window, to lower himself to take it."

Choisy did a little shopping, though he was disappointed at the selection ("To have rare things, you have to be here in the months of April and May, when ships arrive from China and Japan."), and was also given a tour of the royal palace and its adjacent Wat Phra Si Sanphet, where he saw a much-revered Buddha. ("The monks say this image sometimes goes for excursions outside the palace, but the desire to do so only comes when one can see nothing.") At Lop Buri, King Narai's summer retreat, he and the ambassador were put up in a specially built palace with French decorative motifs and attended a hunt for wild elephants. Finally, on 15 December, after a stay of three months, they left Ayutthaya, accompanied by a fleet of royal barges and carrying with them an enormous number of presents for the French court and three Thai envoys.

Unlike their predecessors, the Thai envoys were a social sensation in Paris, their courtly manners praised and their silk costumes so admired they were soon being copied by French manufacturers. Otherwise, however, they accomplished little of substance; the real negotiations, involving the wily Tachard, were going on behind their backs and amounted to something very close to the idea of French domination in Siam, not only religious but also commercial and military.

A second embassy led by Simon de la Loubère, a talented writer of light verse in his spare time, left for Siam in March of 1687. It was very different from Chaumont's: this time there were five ships and a total of 1,361 persons, including almost 500 soldiers and 15 Jesuits led by Tachard, and instead of good will it would bring disaster to both King Narai and Phaulkon within a year.

must admit I was most embarrassed. I did not know what advice to give him. I thought of carrying the Ambassador's chair near to the throne, so that he could climb up on it, when, suddenly, after having finished his discourse, he made his decision. He moved proudly toward the throne, holding the golden cup in which was the letter, and presented the letter to the King without raising his elbow, as if the King were at the same low level as he. Mr Constance, who was crawling on the floor behind us, cried to the Ambassador, 'Lift it up, lift it up!' but he did no such thing, and the good King was obliged to lean half out of the window to take the letter, which he did laughing. Here is the reason. The King had told Mr Constance, 'I leave you to arrange everything outside, do all that is possible to honour the Ambassador of France; I shall look after the inside.' He did not wish to lower his throne, or to

THE FRENCH envoys and priests who came to Ayutthaya during King Narai's reign were, in the words of Maurice Collis, "the first European gentlemen of quality the Siamese had ever seen". Many of them also wrote accounts of their experiences, and while these vary in quality and objectivity, and must always be read as Western impressions of an alien culture, they provide remarkable glimpses of Thai life at the time.

The most valuable, in the opinion of historians, was La Loubère's *Du Royaume de Siam*, which appeared in 1691. This is ironic in a way since as a diplomat, La Loubère was not a notable success, being haughty and short-tempered, no doubt partly because of Tachard's scheming. Yet he had a keen eye for detail, an intelligent curiosity about the customs he encountered, and recorded what he saw and heard in what remains a classic resource.

He wrote about the food, the houses, the mineral products, the arts, the Buddhist faith, the agriculture, even the comparative charms of Thai and Burmese women. Here are his comments on the latter, as translated by Collis: "There is nothing disreputable about free love in lower-class Siamese opinion. Such love is regarded as a marriage and inconstancy as a divorce. Moreover, Siamese women have naturally such a good opinion of themselves that they do not easily yield to strangers or, at least, do not solicit them. The Burmese women in Siam, as strangers themselves, suit strangers better. Some people are stupid enough to say that they are women of loose character, but the fact is that they want a husband, and when they take a European are faithful to him until he abandons them. If they have children, far from their reputation suffering, their position is assured, and that their so-called husband is white, redounds further to their reputation. It is argued by some observers, who know, that they are more amorous than the Siamese; certainly they are more sprightly and animated."

Nicholas Gervaise, who came as a missionary two years before the Chaumont embassy, was equally informative in his book *The Natural and Political History of the Kingdom of Siam*, published in 1688 and used as a source by La Loubère. He, too, discusses Thai women, in particular a curious concept of beauty:

"One thing that the Siamese ladies cannot endure about us is the whiteness of our teeth, because they believe that the devil has white teeth, and that it is shameful for a human being to have teeth like a beast's. Therefore, as soon as the boys and girls reach the age of fourteen or fifteen, they start trying to make their teeth black and shiny.

PREVIOUS PAGE: *Evening on the Chao Phraya in Ayutthaya.*

THIS PAGE: *Hindu deities among the decorations at Wat Na Phra Men.*

FACING PAGE: *Principal Buddha image at Wat Na Phra Men, dressed in royal attire.*

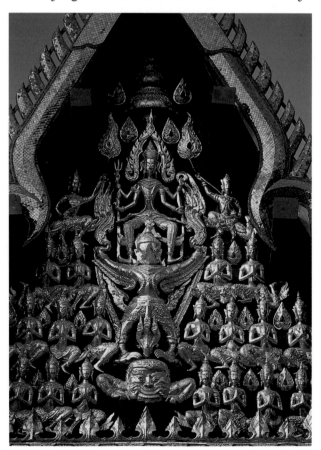

FACING PAGE:
*Buddha images at
Wat Buddhaisawan.*

They do this in the following manner: the person whom they have chosen to render them this service makes them lie down on their back and keeps them in this position for the three days that the operation lasts. First, he cleans the teeth with lemon juice and then having rubbed them with a certain fluid which makes them red, he adds a layer of burnt coconut, which blackens them. The teeth are so weakened by the application of these drugs that they could be extracted painlessly and would even fall out if the patient risked eating any solids, so for these three days he subsists on cold soups, which are fed to him gently so that they flow down his throat without touching the teeth. The least wind could spoil the effect of this operation and that is why the patient stays in bed and makes sure that he is well covered until he feels that it is successfully accomplished by the teeth regaining their firmness in the gums and the disappearance of the swelling of the mouth, which resumes its normal proportions."

Tachard wrote two books, and while he was discreet about his backstage role he seems just as fascinated as the others by the unusual sights he encountered. One was a wild-elephant hunt the ambassadorial party witnessed near Lop Buri:

"Huntsmen go into the woods, mounted on she-elephants which are trained to the game, and cover themselves with leaves of trees that they may not be seen by the wild elephants. When they have got pretty far in the forest, where they think some elephants may be, they make the female give some noise that are proper to attract the males, who presently answer by dreadful roarings. Then the huntsmen, perceiving them at a vast distance, return back again, and gently lead the females toward [a large enclosure]. The wild elephants never fail to follow them. He whom we saw tamed entered with them, and so soon as he was there the bar was shut;

the females kept on their way across the amphitheatre and at one another's tails passed along the little alley that was at the other end. …

"Some Siamese provoked [the wild elephant] by clapping their hands and crying pat, pat, others pricked him with long, sharp, pointed poles, and when they were pursued by him, slipped between the pillars and hid themselves behind the palisades which the elephant could not break through. At length, after having pursued several of the huntsmen, he made at one single man with a great deal of fury. The man ran into the alley and the elephant after him; but as soon as he was within, he was taken for the man, having made his escape, they let fall two [barriers], one before and the other behind the elephant, so that being powerless to go forwards or backwards he struggled prodigiously and made terrible cries. They endeavoured to pacify him by throwing buckets full of water over his body, rubbing him with leaves, pouring oil upon his ears, and they brought tame elephants both males and females to him who caressed him with their trunks. In the meantime, they fastened ropes under his belly and to his hind feet, so that they might pull him out from there, and they persisted in throwing water upon his trunk and body to cool him. …

"They left him there till next day that he might spend his anger; but while he tormented himself around that pillar, a Brahmin (that is to say one of the Indian priests who are numerous in Siam), clothed in white and mounted on another elephant, drew nigh, and … sprinkled him with a certain water consecrated after their manner, which he carried in a vessel of gold. They believe that that ceremony makes the elephant lose his natural fierceness, and fits him to serve the King. The following day he began to go with the rest and in a fortnight's time is fully tamed."

Loy Kratong

Perhaps the loveliest of all water rituals is Loy Krathong, held on a full-moon night at the end of the rains. Countless little banana-leaf boats folded in the shape of lotus blossoms, each adorned with flowers, incense sticks, and a lighted candle, are set adrift in every river and canal to pay homage to the water spirits. Legend claims the ceremony originated at Sukhothai, where a royal consort made the first *krathong*, or lotus-flower boat; but there are older records describing a similar one in the northern Mon city of Haripunchai (Lamphun), where the boats were regarded as a symbolic way of sending gifts to kinsmen in Burma.

FACING PAGE:
Elaborate floats being decorated for the Loy Krathong festival; traditional krathongs *made of folded banana leaf for sale.*

RIGHT: *Scenes of the Loy Krathong celebration in Ayutthaya.*

FOLLOWING PAGES: *People crossing the river with* krathongs *to participate in the annual festival.*

WHEN THEY ARRIVED in September 1687, La Loubère and his party found that Ayutthaya had changed in the three years since Chaumont's visit. A plot to overthrow King Narai had been put down by Phaulkon, some sixty Englishmen had been massacred at Mergui by Thai forces, and anti-foreign sentiment was mounting in conservative circles. Nevertheless, a commercial treaty was signed at the king's palace in Lop Buri and La Loubère left toward the end of December; General Desfarges, in command of the troops, remained behind at the forts in Bangkok, under orders from Phaulkon to hurry to Ayutthaya in case of trouble.

Phaulkon was right to be concerned. In March the king fell desperately ill and the next month open rebellion erupted, led by Phra Phetracha, Commander of the Royal Regiment of Elephants. Phaulkon could probably have escaped but chose to go to the palace in Lop Buri, where he was arrested, tortured for more than a month, and, on 6 June, beheaded on the shore of a nearby lake.

There are various accounts of Phaulkon's death, each reflecting the prejudices of the writer. One is in *Histoire de Monsieur Constance* by a Jesuit priest named Father d'Orleans, so romantically embellished that one later historian suggested a better title might be "Eulogy of a Fictitious Martyr". The inventive Anna Leonowens drew on this for her version, adding such fanciful touches as the idea that King Narai committed suicide just before he was about to be assassinated (in fact, he died a month later):

"Turning from the corpse of the king, the baffled regicides dashed to the luxurious apartment where Phaulkon slumbered, as was his custom of an afternoon, unattended save by his fair young daughter Constantia. Breaking in, they tore the sleeping father from the arms of his agonised child, who with piteous imploring offered her life for his, bound him with cords, dragged him to the woods beyond his garden, and there, within sight of the lovely little Greek chapel he had erected for his private devotions, first tortured him like fiends, and then, dispatching him, flung his body in a pit. His daughter, following them, clung fast to her father, and, though her heart bled and her brain grew numb between the gashes and the groans, she still cheered him with passionate endearments; and, holding before his eyes a cross of gold that always hung on her bosom, inspired him to die like a brave man and a Christian."

Rather different, and probably closer to the truth, is the account written by another Jesuit, Father de Bèze, who was in Ayutthaya during the revolution:

"The courtier came for him at the appointed hour and conducted him on the back of an elephant to the place outside the city which Phetracha had chosen for his execution. Having dismounted Constance went down on his knees — so the courtier informed us — and made protest before God in whose Presence he would soon be standing, that he died innocent of the crimes imputed to him by Phetracha; that the motive of his every action had been to serve and magnify the King, likewise to maintain the throne in the interest of the Royal Family. He then entreated the courtier to have a care for his wife and son, also to protect the poor Christians suffering persecution without just cause. He handed to the courtier the Cross of the Order of St. Michael, requesting him to conserve it for his son until such time as the boy will be of age to carry it for himself as a token of the French king's liking for his father.

"He then put forth his neck beneath the 'Red Arm', who swung the executioner's sword down upon it with a mighty stroke and then with a back-stroke laid open his stomach—as is the custom for those beheaded."

Also according to custom, two younger half-brothers of King Narai were beaten to death with sandalwood clubs wrapped in a velvet sack, and after being crowned king, Phetracha enhanced his legitimacy by marrying Narai's daughter. In Bangkok, General Desfarges held out for another two months, during which he disgraced himself in the eyes of his officers by refusing to help Phaulkon's desperate widow escape; finally he was allowed to withdraw and died on his return trip to France.

Despite these tumultuous events, Ayutthaya did not close its doors to all foreigners. The Dutch retained their factory, which Englebert Kaempfer visited in 1690, and after being briefly imprisoned, the Catholic missionaries resumed their activities; Phaulkon's widow was eventually employed in the royal kitchens, where, according to legend, she introduced a number of still-popular sweets. Rene Charbonneau, a Frenchman who had been medical attendant at a missionary hospital and was later appointed as the Governor of Phuket, returned to the city and spent the remainder of his life there, marrying a girl from the Portuguese community. "Of all the adventurers who came from northern countries in Europe to Siam," wrote E.W. Hutchinson, "he is the only recorded settler in the colonial sense of the term."

After Phetracha's reign, which ended in 1703, Ayutthaya entered a period of unrest and declining power. Struggles for the throne often became violent, and there were periodic threats of civil war, and troubles along the border regions. In 1760, the country was invaded by the Burmese, who almost reached Ayutthaya. This attempt was unsuccessful, but another, six years later, brought disaster to the Thais: after a siege that lasted nearly a year, the capital eventually fell on 7 April 1767.

The Burmese proved merciless. They burned and looted the great capital, carried thousands of captives away to slavery in Burma, and left behind a mass of smouldering ruins. Wyatt cites a contemporary account of a few decades later: "The populace was afflicted with a variety of ills by the enemy. Some wandered about, starving, searching for food. They were bereft of their families, their children and wives, stripped of their possessions and tools. … They gathered in bands and plundered for rice and paddy and salt. Some found food, and others could not. They grew thinner, and their flesh and blood wasted away. Afflicted with a thousand ills, some died and some lived on."

THIS PAGE: *Bell ringer at Wat Buddhaisawan, one of the oldest Ayutthaya temples.* FACING PAGE: *Monks at the same temple.*

FACING PAGE: *People buying freshly cooked noodles from a water-borne vendor in Ayutthaya.*

THIS PAGE: *The* prang *of Wat Chai Wattanaram under recent construction.*

VISITING Ayutthaya's remains in the 1820s, F.A. Neale wrote, "First we come to two stones, one above another, and a small piece of burnt timber, evidently the remains of some house that had caught fire. A few more paces, and we find half a ruined wall, and a lizard (the latter bolted on our near approach); more walls, more stones, more lizards, and then we tumbled across a snake! M___ made short work of him with his gun. The report was the signal for a universal rustling and squealing among the bushes near us. Quadrupeds, bipeds, and insects emerged from their retreat. A jackal and a cat were the next victims to our guns. All this time we marked evident traces of the foundations of houses that had once existed; and the stumps of poles driven fast into the ground led us to understand that these had been the habitations of the poorer class. … Captain S___ picked up the leg of a little statue, beautifully sculpted in marble; but with this exception nothing worthy of note was found."

Other travellers of the time saw piles of rubble ten to twelve feet high, covered with thorny creepers, and half-ruined buildings in which bats and vultures lived; according to Pallegoix, treasure hunters were still digging in the old city, often with success, and people were living both in the ruins and along both sides of the river.

A source cited by Sir John Bowring in 1855 noted the numerous remains that were to be found "hidden in the trees and jungle which have sprung up around them", but went on to describe Ayutthaya as being "the second town of this kingdom" with a population somewhere between twenty and thirty thousand. "They are principally employed in shopkeeping, agriculture, or fishing," he said, "for there are no manufactories of importance. Floating houses are most commonly employed as dwellings, the reason for which is that the Siamese very justly

consider them more healthy than houses on land."

King Mongkut, an enthusiastic student of his country's history, often travelled up the Chao Phraya to the old city, where he built a palace on the river-bank and a rest pavilion in the centre of the ruins. Bowring's informant noted that the king and other nobles annually went to an enormous stockade, or kraal, to view an elephant round-up:

"This is a large quadrangular piece of ground, enclosed by a wall about six feet in thickness, having an entrance on one side, through which the elephants are made to enter the enclosure. Inside the wall is a fence of strong teak stakes driven into

SUCH PEACE is rarer in Ayutthaya today, especially in the modern town, crowded with nondescript shophouses and noisy motorcycles. But on the other side of the island, amid the brooding ruins, some sense of the past can be recaptured despite the presence of souvenir stalls, postcard vendors, and tour buses visiting on day trips from Bangkok, as well as the not always happy efforts at restoration on some temples.

Only the foundations mark the site of the royal palace, originally built in 1448, and one must read such accounts as Choisy's to imagine what it looked like at its peak of splendour. Close by, however, a ruined cloister and three spired stupas that were once part of Wat Phra Si Sanphet, the royal chapel, are still impressive, as is Wat Ratchaburana, with its rounded, Khmer-style *prang*—a symbolic representation of the sacred Mount Meru—where in 1957 excavators found a remarkable trove of more than 2,000 gold objects that had somehow eluded nearly two centuries of treasure hunters.

Though St Joseph's Cathedral, where Roman Catholics worshipped in King Narai's time, still overlooks the river, few traces remain of the once-populous foreign quarter, which Gervaise described as having "quite well-built brick houses" and being "the commercial centre of the kingdom". However, it is probable that a boat-building school—reputedly the last in Thailand to teach the construction of wooden boats—continues to offer classes at or near a site that he called "very convenient for repairing ships, and every day new vessels are built there".

Among the most evocative ruins in Ayutthaya are those of Wat Chai Wattanaram, on the opposite bank of the Chao Phraya as it curves around the less populated part of the island. Con-

LEFT: *A modern barge, of a type rapidly replacing the old teak vessels on the river.*
FACING PAGE: *Wat Chai Wattanaram; across the river can be glimpsed a Thai-style palace presented to Her Majesty the Queen by the Crown Prince on her sixtieth birthday.*

sisting of a central *prang* and other monuments, surrounded by a wall adorned with Buddha images, it was built in 1630 by King Prasat Thong on what had been the site of his mother's palace; fittingly enough, the present Crown Prince recently gave the Queen a Thai-style palace across from the temple on the occasion of her sixtieth birthday. People from Ayutthaya call Wat Chai Wattanaram "the sunset temple" and often come to watch the late afternoon light coat the old stones with a patina of soft gold, while timeless barge processions still move along the river just as they did in the days when Thailand's capital was a renowned centre of culture and busy trade.

Building and repairing boats around Ayutthaya

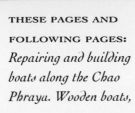

THESE PAGES AND FOLLOWING PAGES: *Repairing and building boats along the Chao Phraya. Wooden boats, now becoming increasingly rare, are still being built at a school in Ayutthaya.*

AYUTTHAYA TO NAKHON SAWAN

"As we proceed onward up stream the flat stretches on each bank are seen to be covered with waving rice fields, while the river is alive with boats, which with their white sails look like huge birds floating on the water. The banks in some places are riddled with holes, the nests of a speckled black and white kingfisher and of a green and rather large species of fly-catcher. These holes go as much as eight feet into the bank. Some are on the perpendicular face of the bank, others are within easy reach of snakes, but the inhabitants tell me that the snakes do not enter the holes, as they are perfectly straight and narrow, and if the snake got in it could not get out. The birds appear perfectly happy, as though they knew no danger, and the two different species seem to live together in harmony and peace. On we go past the white-sailed boats skimming over the water, and we must make the most of our time, as the river each day is falling."

The anonymous author of *An Englishman's Siamese Journals 1890-1893* was between Ayutthaya and Chai Nat, on his way to Chiang Mai in the far north. This was the heart of the old Chao Phraya delta and, until toward the end of the nineteenth century, the principal source of rice and other produce for both Ayutthaya and Bangkok. Mons and Khmers had settled on the fertile river-banks before the Thais established communities of their own in such provinces as Chai Nat, Phitsanulok, and Nakhon Sawan, and the northernmost section had been part of Sukhothai, the first independent Thai kingdom. During the Ayutthaya period, most of the population also lived along this stretch of the river, the young delta below being largely a wilderness except for a few ports and special places, covered with water in the flood season.

Though there must have been considerable boat traffic, bringing food and people to the capital, no Ayutthayan descriptions of the route survive. Excursions seem to have mainly been by the much smaller Lop Buri River to the city of the same name, where King Narai maintained his summer palace, or by the Pasak to a landing from which pilgrimages were made overland to the sacred Buddha's Footprint called Phra Phutthabat.

Similarly, few foreign visitors travelled very far up-river above the old capital until the 1830s, and for a century or so afterwards those who did

FACING PAGE: *An old engraving showing the flooded Chao Phraya delta, an annual phenomenon at the end of the rainy season.*
THIS PAGE: *An imaginative version of a Thai house, from Simon de la Loubère's account of his visit to seventeenth-century Ayutthaya.*

FOLLOWING PAGES: *Schoolchildren disembarking from a ferry at Wat Chai Yo, a Rattanakosin-style temple in Ang Thong province.*

were generally on their way to more interesting northern experiences and left sparse accounts of their impressions along the way. Carl Bock, for instance, has only the following to say about what he saw in 1883 between Ayutthaya and Nakhon Sawan, where the Chao Phraya begins:

"Every few miles the banks are dotted with villages, the river flowing through a low alluvial plain, thickly populated, and studded with temples and prachedees [*chedis*] whose conical spires serve to relieve the monotony of the scenery. The country is very fertile, but from the river no sign of cultivation can be seen, the rice-fields lying out of sight at a short distance from the banks, behind the villages and the forest-growth.

"As we proceeded up stream the river gradually became shallower and frequently obstructed by sand banks. It was the dry season, the effect of which was seen, not only in the rapidly decreasing volume of water, but in the shrivelled appearance of the foliage, which was beginning to lose its brilliant, glossy green hue."

Today, as in the past, the scenery along the river alters as one moves up into the old delta, even though the actual elevation remains slight—Ayutthaya, a hundred kilometres inland, is only two metres above sea-level. The banks become steeper, with a well-worn path leading down to the water from each house, and are lined with trees and huge clumps of bamboo that conceal both villages and fields; in the dry months, as Bock noted, sand bars make navigation tricky for larger boats, and the main channel is sometimes only around 120 centimetres deep, marked with a variety of signs to indicate directions and danger points. A diversity of crops is being grown, however, thanks to major irrigation projects begun only in the 1950s: rice, of course, but also tapioca (sacks of the white flour

being loaded onto barges from riverside processing plants), fruit trees, toddy palms, and gourds stretched over bamboo frames on the sandy beaches.

The first important town is Ang Thong, an ancient settlement through which the Burmese marched during their final assault on Ayutthaya in 1767. Bishop Pallegoix, who visited the town in 1831, got the name wrong and called it Hang Thong ("golden tail"), which he later corrected to the proper one, meaning "golden pot". A few years later, Dr Bradley stopped there and made a different kind of mistake, assuming from the few simple houses he saw that it was poor and sparsely populated; only when he explored further did he realise that it was in fact of considerable size.

North of Ang Thong, numerous temples can be seen on both banks of the river, by far the most impressive being Wat Chai Yo Vora Viharn. Built in Rattanakosin style and overlooking the water from the top of a high embankment of cement and stone, this temple enjoys the patronage of many wealthy people from Bangkok who have donated funds not only for its lavish decorations but also for a partially completed bridge across the Chao Phraya to facilitate travel by car from the main northern highway. Inside, along with an enormous seated Buddha image, are statues and portraits of King Chulalongkorn, currently the object of cult worship among a certain segment of city people.

At Sing Buri, formerly known as Muang Sing, forty-odd kilometres above Ang Thong, the river becomes increasingly shallow and there are few large vessels, mainly small boats and dug-out canoes. There are no bridges, and both people and vehicles cross the river by ferries going back and forth regularly throughout the day. In Pallegoix's time, the town was almost entirely Chinese, including the governor, and had a large distillery producing

rice whiskey; on the west bank there were dense forests and, along the river, tiger tracks. Most of the forests (and the tigers) have vanished today, and villages can be located behind their bamboo groves by a taller thicket of television aerials.

The town of In Buri overlooks the river twenty kilometres north. Here Pallegoix found a Thai governor and a mixed population of Thais, Laos, and Chinese who lived in houses strung out

for a considerable distance and earned a living from the cultivation of rice, areca palm, cotton, and sugar-cane.

Between In Buri and Chai Nat, the river-banks are sparsely populated, as they were when Pallegoix came, and though one no longer sees the numerous crocodiles that he noted on the muddy shores, kingfishers keep watch on the shallow water and swoop down in a flash of brilliant blue whenever an unwary snack swims past. Then houses, temples, and boat traffic steadily increase and, rounding a bend, the massive bulk of the Chai Nat Dam, first of its kind in Thailand, looms suddenly into view.

The dam was the ultimate result of more than half a century of proposals and plans. In 1888, as we have seen in a previous chapter, the Siam Canals, Land and Irrigation Company was established to open lands of the lower delta to rice culture to meet the demand created by trade treaties signed with Western countries. A Department of Canals was founded by the government in 1899 and given responsibility for proposing a far more ambitious scheme, covering the upper Chao Phraya as well.

The first director-general of the new department was a Dutchman named Homan van der Heide, who had had extensive experience of such work in his home country. He spent a decade in the post during which he devised a programme that, in the words of Yoshikazu Takaya, "was more than just an irrigation and drainage plan; in modern terms it was a piece of regional planning". Among other things, it proposed that a dam be built across the Chao Phraya at Chai Nat; the water level of the main stream would thus be raised, some of the water being used for irrigation in the old delta and the rest being conveyed by a canal system to the young delta at a raised level, high enough to allow gravity flow

and deep enough for the passage of boats through the network.

Van der Heide never saw the implementation of his great plans. At the time the government was spending vast sums on railway construction, regarded as more vital to the country's future, and most of his proposals were either rejected or postponed. Only after the Second World War, when international food shortages revealed the potential value of the Chao Phraya delta, was the concept revived. The Greater Chao Phraya Project, begun in the 1950s with assistance from the World Bank, finally resulted in the Chai Nat Dam—237.5 metres long, with a series of sixteen sluice gates—and transformed the delta into the fertile resource envisioned by van der Heide fifty years before.

In the early 1960s, the Bhumibol Dam—a semi-circle of cement 154 metres high and 486 metres long, one of the largest of its kind in Asia—was constructed on the Ping River near Tak, primarily for generating electricity but also to control flooding; and this was followed in 1973 by the Sirikit Dam across the Nan River, another of the Chao Phraya's tributaries, in Uttaradit Province.

The dams, and the regulated water supplies they made possible, transformed agriculture and life styles in the region. Now, except in periods of severe drought, farmers can grow two and sometimes even three rice crops a year, as well as a diversity of other commercial plants not possible before. "The traditional raised houses," Takaya notes, "have begun to be replaced by ground-level Western-style houses with lawns and gardens, as if people expected there never again to be flooding." Moreover, the system of irrigation canals has also improved transport and communication, while the electric power generated has brought countless innovations to once isolated villages.

PREVIOUS PAGES:
Houses along Klong Manohra, a waterway leading off the Chao Phraya; a new bridge under construction in Ang Thong; and a riverside town studded with television aerials.
RIGHT:
The Chai Nat Dam, which was built in the 1950s and revolutionised agriculture in the Chao Phraya delta.

A rice farmer's cycle

It would be almost impossible to overestimate the importance of rice in Thai life. Since the latter part of the nineteenth century, it has been a major source of foreign exchange; in one form or another, it appears on the table of every meal; *kin khao*, the Thai expression for "to eat", literally means "to eat rice".

Rice is grown in every region, from small northern valleys to the southern peninsula, but by far the most plentiful source is the fertile Chao Phraya delta, where a jigsaw pattern of fields and irrigation canals stretches to the horizon in all directions. Here the cycle of its cultivation forms the basic structure of rural existence, determining both work schedules and leisure activities.

The planting season is in April or May, just before the annual rains begin. Its commencement is officially signalled by the Ploughing Ceremony, an ancient Brahmanic ritual that goes back to Ayutthayan times and which was revived by H.M. the present King early in his reign. Today it is held every May at Sanam Luang, the large field across from the Grand Palace in Bangkok, and includes white oxen, Brahmin priests, and a variety of rites believed to forecast the abundance of the coming rice crop. Farmers, especially from the central region, attend the ceremony in large numbers, and many join in the dash for seeds sown by the priests to mix with their own as a kind of blessing.

Work in the fields now begins to intensify. Farmers join in cooperative groups to repair bunds along the irrigation canals, plough the earth with buffaloes or modern tractors, and flood the fields with water from the rising rivers. Meanwhile, young rice seedlings have been started in prepared areas, and when the fields are ready every able-bodied member of the family helps transplant them. The task goes on from early morning until dark and is completed by the time rainfall becomes regular in July.

For the next three months, while the rice is turning from vibrant acid green to a darker shade and beginning to produce its waving heads of grain, the principal village chores consist of keeping birds away and catching fish—the other staple of the Thai diet—in swollen ponds and waterways. Some young men choose this relatively quiet time to enter the local Buddhist monastery, thus fulfilling a basic rite of passage and also bringing merit to their parents.

By November, the rains have stopped and the rice is ready to be harvested. This, too, is a cooperative effort that goes on from early morning until evening. The cut rice is spread in the fields to dry for several days, then tied in sheaves and taken to the family compound for threshing and winnowing before being sold to middlemen or government agencies.

Once the cycle ended here, totally dependent on rainfall. Today reservoirs and the vast irrigation system that extends throughout the delta have made it possible to plant a second rice crop during the dry season. If this is done, the same process is repeated, one as old as Thailand itself and as essential to its ancient culture.

BELOW: *Egrets in the central plains rice fields.* FACING PAGE: *The timeless cycle of rice cultivation, from planting through harvest and then drying paddy before it is milled.*

LEFT: *Trapping fish in an irrigation canal; a farmer rides to work across one of the countless canals that supply water to the rice fields of central Thailand.*

RIGHT: *Children at play on a rural canal.*
FOLLOWING PAGES: *Farmer watering a patch of gourds, one of the many subsidiary crops grown in the delta; and cowherds tending a herd of cattle.*

BEFORE THE DAMS, among the most dramatic sights along the Chao Phraya were the vast rafts of teak logs being floated down to Bangkok. The logs belonged to one of the several firms, mostly foreign, who had received lucrative timber concessions from the government, and their long journey had begun in the once-dense forests of the far north.

After reaching a diameter of at least sixty centimetres, when they were about 150 years old, the teak trees were incised with an axe and then left standing for two years to die and dry out, since newly cut teak would sink when put in water. After being felled, they were trimmed of small branches and cut into logs, which in turn were dragged by elephants to the nearest river or stream and individually floated down to an assembly point to be tied into rafts. There were such points on the Ping, the Yom, and the Nan, all of which join at some place to form the Chao Phraya, and the size of the rafts varied with the river. On the relatively wide Ping, for example, rafts were composed of as many as 350 to 400 logs, while on the winding Yom they had only around 200.

Each raft was literally a floating home, with rudders, a look-out tower, and crew quarters, for the journey downstream was slow and the rafts were often stranded for months in the dry season; some of the heaviest logs took as long as twelve years to reach their destination, while the average time from felling to Bangkok saw mill was between four and five years. The long period in water in no way harmed the timber, indeed it made it harder and even more durable; but there was constant danger of logs being stolen, and their attendants had to be alert all the way.

At Paknam Po, as the junction of rivers at Nakhon Sawan was called, the logs were examined and measured, and duty was collected by an office of the Royal Forestry Department. In 1904, some 100,000 logs were arriving annually at the station. Since the Bangkok mills could not accommodate so many, the rafts ended their journey just above the capital, and smaller quantities were towed down to the capital as needed.

Teak production reached a peak in 1931, with around thirteen million cubic feet felled, but due to a lack of reforestation had dropped to less than half that figure by the mid-1960s; toward the end of the 1980s, all logging was officially ended, though one still sees smaller rafts floating downriver on their way to the comparatively few mills that remain.

Traditional Thai house

In Ang Thong, not far from the provincial capital, stands a traditional Thai house of unusual size, made entirely of teak and displaying refined construction. This is the home of Khun Samruey Rueycharong, an imaginative entrepreneur who also uses it as a model for customers entranced by the classic style and seeking a similar structure of their own.

A simpler version of such a house was described by one Western visitor early in the present century as consisting of "a platform of teak planks ... supported on piles, six or seven feet above the ground, and approached by a ladder leading down into the klong. Opening on to two sides of the platform are little houses, also built of teak, with graceful gable ends curving upward to a sharp point. ... The platform is often gay with flowering shrubs, amongst which brilliant butterflies flit about. It forms the courtyard, from which it is only a step up to the floors of the houses. The sleeping-rooms are at the back, but in front and open to the platform are deep verandahs, in which the family live during the day."

This traditional Thai house is a model of airy elegance and down-to-earth practicality. With its whimsically curved eaves, steep roof, and walls that lean slightly inward, it seems to be straining toward the sky, about to take off from the tall pillars on which it perches. At the same time, it is artfully designed to catch any passing breeze, while the open area below is convenient for keeping domestic animals and tools. Since most of the components are prefabricated and joined only with wooden pegs, it can be easily dismantled from the frame, stacked on a barge or cart, and moved to a new location whenever the need arises.

Once such houses were as much a part of the Thai scene as the more ornate Buddhist temples, both on land and, in a slightly different form, floating along river-banks. With the spread of Western tastes and cheaper building materials, however, their appeal waned, especially in large cities like Bangkok. Only in relatively recent years has there been a revival of interest in them, to such a degree that Khun Samruey's carpenters must now work overtime to keep up with the demand.

Components from her shop have been assembled in dozens of Bangkok compounds, either simple structures used mainly for entertaining or more complex ones adapted for modern city life. The firm has also dispatched builders to Monte Carlo, where they assembled a pavilion ordered by a wealthy resident, and not long ago they constructed a group of ten houses which will eventually rise beside the sea in Hawaii.

THIS PAGE: *The owner of S. Rueycharong, a business in Ang Thong that has built many traditional Thai houses for contemporary admirers of the classic style.*

FACING PAGE: *Home of the owner, from which prospective buyers can select features that appeal to them.*

FOLLOWING PAGES: *Various components of Thai-style houses and decorations under construction.*

DESPITE an illustrious history going back to the twelfth century and including a period as a dependency of the Sukhothai kingdom, Nakhon Sawan was almost deserted when Pallegoix visited it in 1834. Crocodiles slept undisturbed on the river-banks, and the town had only about a hundred houses, none of them impressive; the days of its central role in the teak trade still lay ahead, and it was a place to pause only briefly before heading further north by either the Ping River or the Nan.

Today, any crocodiles encountered are likely to be at Bung Boraphet, an extensive reservoir about a kilometre up the Nan which varies in size according to the season and which has been established as a fish and aquatic bird preserve. Nakhon Sawan itself has become a bustling provincial capital on the right bank, its commercial importance based not only on the river traffic but also on goods that pass through by road and railway. There are tall buildings, a busy market, a scenic public park, a riverside promenade along which to stroll in the evening, and atop a lofty hill overlooking the town, a temple enshrines a sacred Buddha's Footprint from the Sukhothai period.

Near the market one can hire a boat and, halfway across, pause at the precise spot where the Chao Phraya originates. Except in the very driest months, this is vividly evident. From the northwest flows the Ping, usually bright green, and from the northeast the reddish Nan, which further north has been joined by the Yom. The two rivers meet at a narrow spit of land, blend their contrasting colours, and then, as the Chao Phraya, begin the sinuous course southward to the gulf.

Neither Pallegoix nor any other early visitor seems to have been particularly impressed by the sight; and, in truth, one has to admit that it is lacking in the drama, the sense of momentous dis-covery, associated with other great river sources. After all, even against a strong current toward the end of the rainy season, Nakhon Sawan can be reached from Bangkok in three or four days by boat, allowing for overnight stops on the way; and by road it is a matter of but a few hours.

Only when one takes time to reflect on what the Chao Phraya has meant throughout recorded Thai history, on the role it continues to play, does the confluence at Nakhon Sawan assume real significance. Then, one remembers how for centuries the broad stream that begins so mundanely here has brought nourishment to the countless fields below and prosperity to the cities which rose along its banks, how it has also served as a highway for trade and transforming new ideas, how much modern Thais still depend on it for countless everyday needs perhaps unrealised by many of them. And, recalling all this, one begins to understand why it remains truly a great river of life as well as legend.

BELOW: *Marker in a shallow stretch of the Chao Phraya to indicate the main channel.*
FACING PAGE: *An overview of the river at Nakhon Sawan.*

Traditional crafts

FACING PAGE AND ABOVE: *Various village crafts in production, among them miniature dolls, baskets, and drums. Made by traditional methods, these are finding new buyers in cities far from the rural areas.*

LEFT: *The point at which the Ping and Nan rivers meet at Nakhon Sawan to form the Chao Phraya.*

ABOVE: *Lotus being cultivated for flowers, seed, and leaves along the river.*

Bibliography

Anonymous, *An Englishman's Siamese Journals 1890-1893* (reprint by Siam Media International Books, Bangkok, n.d.)

Antonio, J., *Guidebook to Bangkok and Siam, 1904* (Siam Observer Press, Bangkok, 1904).

Beauvoir, Marquis de, *A Week in Siam, January 1867* (The Siam Society, Bangkok, 1986).

Berlingieri, Giorgio, *An Oriental Album* (D.K. Book House, Bangkok, n.d.).

Bock, Carl, *Temples and Elephants* (reprint by White Lotus Press, Bangkok, 1985).

Bowring, Sir John, *The Kingdom and the People of Siam* (reprint by Oxford University Press, Kuala Lumpur, 1969).

Bradley, William L., *Siam Then* (William Carey Library, Pasadena, 1981).

Bristowe, W.S., *Louis and the King of Siam* (Thai-American Publishers, New York, 1978).

Bryant, Nancy, "Water Spirits" *Sawaddi Magazine*, (American Women's Club, Bangkok, July-August 1968).

Caddy, Mrs. Florence, *To Siam and Malaya* (Hurst and Blackett, Ltd., London, 1889).

Choisy, Abbé de, *Journal of a Voyage to Siam*, translated by Michael Smithies (Oxford University Press, Kuala Lumpur, 1993).

Chou Ta-Kuan, *The Customs of Cambodia* (The Siam Society, Bangkok, 1987).

Chu, Valentine, *Thailand Today* (Thomas Y. Crowell Company, New York, 1968).

Collis, Maurice, *Siamese White* (Faber and Faber, London, 1936).

Crawfurd, John, *Journal of an Embassy to the Courts of Siam and Cochin China* (Oxford University Press, Kuala Lumpur, 1967)

Gervaise, Nicholas, *The Natural and Political History of the Kingdom of Siam* (reprint by White Lotus Press, Bangkok, 1989).

Griswold, Alexander B., *King Mongkut of Siam* (The Asia Society, New York, 1961).

Hunter, Kay, *Duet for a Lifetime* (Michael Joseph, London, 1964).

Hutchinson, R.W., *Adventurers in Siam in the Seventeenth Century* (reprint by DD Books, Bangkok, 1985).

Kaempfer, Englebert, *A Description of the Kingdom of Siam, 1690* (reprint by White Orchid Press, Bangkok, 1987).

M.R. Kukrit Pramoj, *Si Phaendin*, English version by Tulachandra (Editions Duang Kamol, Bangkok, n.d.).

La Loubère, Simon, *A New Historical Relation of the Kingdom of Siam* (reprint by Chalermnit, Bangkok, n.d.).

Leonowens, Anna, *The English Governess at the Siamese Court* (reprint by Chalermnit, Bangkok, n.d.).

Lord, Donald C., *Mo Bradley and Thailand* (William R. Eerdmans Publishing Company, Grand Rapids, 1969).

Maugham, Somerset, *The Gentleman in the Parlour* (William Heinemann Ltd., London, 1930).

National Identity Board, *Thailand in the 80s* (Office of the Prime Minister, Bangkok, 1984).

Neale, F.A., *Narrative of a Residence in Siam* (Reprint by White Orchid Press, Bangkok).

Plion-Bernier, Raymond, *Festivals and Ceremonies of Thailand* (Assumption Press, Bangkok, 1973).

Portugal, Embassy of, *Thailand and Portugal: 476 Years of Friendship* (Calouste Gulbenkian Foundation, Lisbon, 1987).

Rong Syamananda, *A History of Thailand* (Thai Watana Panich Co. Ltd., Bangkok, 1973).

M.R. Seni Pramoj and M.R. Kukrit Pramoj, *A King of Siam Speaks* (The Siam Society, Bangkok, 1987).

Smith, Malcolm, *A Physician at the Court of Siam* (Oxford University Press, Kuala Lumpur, 1982).

Sthirakoses (Phraya Anuman Rajdhon), *Looking Back* (Chulalongkorn University Press, Bangkok, 1992).

Sumet Jumsai, Thongthong Chandransu, M.R. Chakarot Chitrabongs, and Khunying Chamnongsri, *Royal Barges: Poetry in Motion* (Office of the Prime Minister, Bangkok, n.d.).

Tachard, Guy, *Voyage to Siam 1685* (reprint by White Orchid Press, Bangkok 1981).

Takaya, Yoshikazu, *Agricultural Development of a Tropical Delta: A Study of the Chao Phraya Delta* (University of Hawaii Press, Honolulu, 1987).